Lord, Are You Sure?

by *Marnie L. Pehrson*

Copyright 2003 Marnie L. Pehrson
All Rights Reserved

Cover Photo by Al Hollis,
Cover Design by Tamara Ingram

Published by CES Business Consultants
514 Old Hickory Ln * Ringgold GA 30736
Tel: 706-866-2295
www.SheLovesGod.com

ISBN: 0-9729750-0-4

*Dedicated to my dear friends
from whom I've learned so much:
Alanna, Debbie, Jenette,
Karon and Leslie*

Table of Contents

Introduction 5

Chapter 1: An Aerial View 12

Chapter 2: Is This Treasure On Your List? 27

Chapter 3: Faith: The Stuff From Which Treasures Are Made 48

Chapter 4: Gratitude: The Key That Unlocks the Treasury of Heaven 63

Chapter 5: Your Navigating Co-Pilot 77

Chapter 6: Are You Going in Circles? 91

Chapter 7: Cast Thy Bread Upon the Waters 107

Chapter 8: Cast Not Away Thy Confidence 113

Chapter 9: The Due Time of the Lord 123

Chapter 10: Amazing Grace 139

Conclusion 145

Introduction

> *"Lay up for yourselves treasures in heaven where neither moth nor rust doth corrupt, and where thieves do not break through nor steal."* Matthew 6:20

One of the hardest things for a Christian to understand is what God is up to in his/her life. We go through spiritual highs and lows, have challenges and afflictions, suffer and sometimes succumb to temptation. All of this can seem confusing at times. Isn't following God supposed to be joyous and froth with continual blessings? On the contrary, the Christian life is hardly a free hopper pass to Disney World. Christian or not, life is difficult, demanding and sometimes downright unfair. But if we can find the meaning in it all, it's much easier to bear, and we'll have peace knowing that God knows where He's taking us and that the journey will all be worth it.

God works in definite patterns in the lives of His children. Understand His methods and how He navigates, and you begin to see what He is trying to teach you. You may think He's crazy stopping off to see the largest ball of twine, until a piece of that twine comes in handy on a later adventure. Everything He does is for a reason, and that reason is to prepare you for something later down the road. Understanding human nature and also how God disciplines and instructs his children will help you quit questioning His navigation. You'll begin to relax and let God work His wonder in your life.

When we don't understand what He's doing, we have a tendency to loose faith and have difficulty trusting. If you don't understand the road signs and landscape of your journey, you'll be continually questioning His directions. In essence, you'll be saying, "Lord, are you sure we're on the right road? Maybe I should navigate for a while."

Have you ever said to yourself, "When I grow up, I'll be able to do this or that" or "When I get married, everything will be perfect." Or "When I finish college…" Or "When I'm financially independent…" Or "When I retire…" Most of us are always putting off happiness or "success" until the next big event we're approaching. And if that event doesn't occur - say something happens and you don't get married or graduate from college or have children or reach that career goal – then somehow you think you've failed. You might think God has let you down because you haven't achieved a package of "success" that other people have attained. You've been deprived.

I like to think of life as a long distance treasure hunt where we travel the countryside sometimes by plane, car or boat and collect treasures. Some people spend more effort collecting earthly treasures while others focus on heavenly ones. Jesus said, "Lay up for yourselves treasures in heaven where moth nor rust doth corrupt and where thieves do not break through and steal." Many people spend their lives collecting treasures that will not last beyond mortality. Others realize that there are two important types of heavenly treasures that we can take back home with us. These two are the wisdom and knowledge we attain and the relationships we develop. These are the only things we can take with us.

There's a Southern saying: "I never saw a hearse pullin' a u-haul." It's not the wealth we accumulate or the positions of power or authority we attain that go home with us; it is who we become that counts. The treasury of memories, knowledge, wisdom, experience and love we collect forges into our souls and fashions us into the person Heavenly Father sent us here to become.

Each of us has a unique custom-designed list of treasures to collect on our treasure hunt. This is because no two of us enter this life with identical personalities or spirits. Each spirit needs a different set of circumstances and opportunities to develop as God intends. My list will be different than yours. Yours will be different than your best friend's. But each list is absolutely perfect for each one of us. Just

because your best friend got married and had six children and seemingly "lived happily ever after" doesn't mean that your life is a failure if you don't encounter the same events. Your treasure list might take you on a much different path – one that does not entail marriage or children but may involve a life of service in a career path.

The worst thing you can do is to compare your list with your neighbor's. His or her list is no more appropriate or successful than yours. The only important thing is that you are gathering the list of treasures that the Lord gave you to collect. Success or failure is not measured in comparison with others, only in whether you collected the treasures that were assigned you.

When we begin to compare lists with others, we start questioning whether God really has our best interests at heart. We begin to question whether God knows what He is doing or whether somehow we're doing something wrong because our list is very different than the next guy's. We have the intense desire to take over the navigation of the plane, car or boat and start steering it to match someone else's list. While we're off chasing someone else's treasures, we're not gathering the ones that are custom-made for us.

It's like spending all your time and money to save up for a pair of shoes that are two sizes too small. They may be nice and expensive, but they don't fit you. You can't wear them. You'd be better off with a less expensive set of comfortable shoes that fit your feet perfectly.

Another similarity between life and a treasure hunt is that the order you collect your treasures may not matter in the least. I collected my treasure of marriage when I was 19. Another person may not acquire hers until she is 65. Your friend may have a career while she's in her twenties; yours may wait until after your children leave home. It really doesn't matter when you attain the items on your list, just so long as you collect them. The only importance time plays is that you don't want to squander your life away – out of God's will – and wait until you are 85 to start collecting. Odds are that you won't be able to gather a lifetime of treasures in a few short years.

In this book, we'll discuss ways to recognize the treasures that the Lord has in store for you. You'll learn how to trust not only that the Lord has your best interest in mind, but also that you will enjoy the journey and the treasures you gather. You'll also learn more about how to trust God's timing. He sometimes delivers on a different timetable than you'd like, but if the treasure's on your list, it will be delivered.

Chapter 1
An Aerial View

"All things work together for good to them that love God, to them that are the called according to His purpose." - Romans 8:28

I had been on a spiritual "high" for nearly two years. Everything was smooth sailing when suddenly in June of 2002 an obstacle landed across my path that brought my world to a screeching halt. Just when I thought I'd found my way, an old familiar challenge reared its ugly head. "Haven't I learned this lesson already? Do I really need to go through this *again?*" I asked myself. But there it was, bigger than life, a huge boulder obstructing the path that I felt certain God wanted me to travel.

Within a few days of learning that I was to face, yet again, an obstacle that I knew all too well, I boarded a plane to see a dear friend in Florida. The first leg of the trip was from Chattanooga to Charlotte in a small prop plane.

As we rose into the air and glided across the Tennessee Valley landscape, the aerial view afforded me a different perspective of the city I'd called home my entire life.

Two speedboats curled their way through the river's path, veering closely to one another and then away - seconds before colliding. The highways stretched for miles, meandering through the countryside. From my perspective, I could see the traffic jams farther down roads that cars wouldn't reach for miles ahead. I could see detours long before earthbound travelers would ever encounter them. If there had been a fallen tree blocking a path, it would have been clearly visible from my aerial view.

I began to ponder on this vantage point, and thought, "This is how God sees my life. He's up high where the view is clear. He knows if someone else's poor choices are about to crash into my world. He sees the detours, traffic jams and trees thrown across my path miles before I'll ever reach them." And then the realization struck me with such force. My Father in Heaven had been preparing me for the last few years to face this challenge. He knew it was coming. He knew what was happening behind the scenes that I could not see. And He was doing everything within His power to build my faith, strengthen my trust in Him, and prepare me for the detour that would lie ahead. What a feeling of peace and love filled my soul when I understood that everything was within His hands and that He loved me enough to prepare me years in advance for a challenge I wouldn't face for miles ahead!

The remainder of the trip gave time to step back from my problems enough to see them in their proper perspective. They still seemed formidable and I had no idea how I would face them or fix them, but I knew that the Lord would carry me through. The answers would come when the time was right.

Upon landing in Ft. Lauderdale, I was greeted by a friend who had been instrumental in my spiritual growth in recent years. Instrumental, actually, would be a weak word for the transformation the Savior made in both our lives through this friendship. I found it no small coincidence that at the beginning of a difficult journey, the Lord carried me 900 miles to spend a few days with this wise and dear friend. I had come full circle.

In so many ways our lives travel in circles. There's something that God loves about circles. The earth spins on its axis in a circular motion; it revolves around the Sun in an elliptical path; the shape of the planets are spherical. It seemed only fitting that the Lord took me full circle to the person who initiated my last phase of spiritual development to close that segment of my life and inaugurate a new adventure. The poetry, timing and intricacy of the Lord's dealings in our minuscule lives always astounds me. This trip was just further evidence of that fact.

Away from the harried life of a mother of six and small business owner, and relaxing in the quiet world of my friend who was in the first few months of motherhood, gave me a place to reflect, read, ponder and pray. Originally the only solution I could find for the financial crisis which had struck our family, was to sell my largest and most profitable Web site. My former coach was able to ask key questions to help me evaluate the situation from the outside looking in. Through her questions, I came to realize that this was not the solution to my problem. For in selling this site, I would undermine the fabric of my business and lose the one automated flow of income that gave me time to spend with my family. My friend helped me see that the sale of this site would require the sacrifice of something dear – the sacrifice of the time I spend with my family. This was a sacrifice I was not prepared to make. Through prayer, I soon learned that this was not a sacrifice that the Lord wished me to make.

After ruling out the only solution I could think of I began my search for another one. The second morning in Florida, I awoke with a clear and definite answer. I was to sell a smaller site and was given some clear ideas about who to approach and how to sell it. I had such an overwhelming feeling of peace and gratitude about this solution. That is where I would start when I returned home.

The next couple days passed quickly and I was on a plane heading back to reality. How thankful I am that the Lord gave me a momentary view from his perspective and the time in quiet contemplation to rejuvenate and fortify myself in the eye before the storm!

Upon returning, I immediately followed through on the leads and ideas I had for selling the Web site. But it didn't sell. No one wanted it - even though it had great potential within the hands of the people I approached. As I researched more people to talk to about buying the site, I began to see that there were ways that I could increase the revenues from this site that I had never tried before. I saw opportunities that had been there all along, but which I had never seen or pursued.

I began pursuing these and shortly thereafter the site began to increase in revenue, bringing much-needed funds into our family resources. Day by day I began to act upon ideas for generating more revenue from my Web sites and through the grace of God I was able to earn the money our family needed to more than meet our monthly obligations.

Everyone has their crosses to carry - their adversities to endure and overcome. As the stormy waves have dashed across the bow of my ship, I have learned that faith in our Heavenly Father and His Son, Jesus Christ is the only anchor strong enough to hold you steady in the waves of adversity. The following are 12 tools for keeping your faith centered in Christ so you can have peace even amidst the winds and the waves.

Take time every day to pray, read your scriptures, and meditate. By meditate I mean take some quiet time without worry or angst and just listen to the still small voice. Many times our solutions are right in front of us, but we can't see them because our cries for help or the busyness of life deafen us to the still small voice. Take time to listen each day.

Take it one day at a time. As Matthew 6:34 says, "Take therefore no thought for the morrow:

for the morrow shall take thought for the things of itself." Now, we do have to prepare for the future, but fretting about tomorrow is fruitless. Praise Him for what He's given you today - no matter how meager. Don't whine to Him about tomorrow or this month or the next. Just ask Him each morning for what you have need of today. You can also ask Him for what you need by a certain date. But if you find yourself getting too anxious, worried or whiny about not having enough to meet next week's challenges, step back and only look at what you need today, and usually you'll find that He has provided for the needs of the day. Make a point to be grateful for today.

Don't hide your head in the sand. Sometimes it's human nature to hide from our problems. For example, if you are in the middle of a financial crunch, you might have a tendency to put bills out of site and refuse to look at them so that you don't have to worry about them. This is a dangerous trap. Don't hide from your problems. Face them head-on in faith with the Lord at your side. Assess the situation. In the financial example, write down everything you owe for the month and the absolute last date it needs to be mailed in order to be paid on time. It helps to sort it in order by date. Then pray over the list and tell the Lord that you're giving it to Him to handle. You have to be honest about where you are if you want to get where you're going. If you are in Atlanta and you're trying to get to Disney World, but you're telling yourself you're in Miami, you're going to have a tough time finding your way. Be honest with yourself and with God about where you are. And if you're not certain where you are, ask Him!

Use visual methods to give your challenges to God. For example, I've found it helpful in tight money situations to keep the family budget behind a picture of Jesus Christ holding a little white lamb that sits on my desk. That picture reminds me that Christ has us safely in His arms. He's not going to drop us. Each morning, I would pull that list out from behind the picture of Christ, see what was due, ask the Lord for it if I didn't have it and thank Him in advance, because I knew He'd provide it. If I did have it, I'd pay those bills and thank Him for the ability to do so. Then back the list would go behind His picture. You can use this with any problem you may have. Put something that symbolizes your troubles behind a picture of Christ and let Him carry your burden (Matthew 11:29).

If you catch yourself doubting or worrying. STOP. Pull out your scriptures, put on some hymns or praise music, drop to your knees and ask for the strength to have faith. Thank Him for what you do have and what you know He will deliver (Matthew 21:21).

Center your faith in Christ, not your outcome. Christ is a firm and solid foundation on which we can build. As a wise man once told his sons, "Remember that it is upon the rock of our Redeemer, who is Christ, the Son of God, that ye must build your foundation; that when the devil sends forth his mighty winds, his shafts in the whirlwind, when all his hail and his mighty storm shall beat upon you, it shall have no power over you to drag you down to the gulf of misery and endless wo, because of the rock upon which you are built, which is a sure foundation, a foundation whereon if men and women build they cannot fail." Don't build your faith on the outcome you want, rather pray, "Be it unto me according to my faith in Christ." Read Matthew 14:22-33 about

Jesus walking on the water and Peter taking a few steps on the water. There are great lessons here. The men were scared that Jesus was a ghost and were afraid. Sometimes the things that look the very worst coming toward us are for our greatest good. When Peter kept His eyes on Christ, he could walk on water. When he became fearful and distracted by the winds and the waves, he began to sink. Keep your eye on the Master.

Open Your Mind and Heart. The Lord may provide for you in a way or means you never even considered. His outcome for you may be something different than you had in mind. But rest assured that "all things work together for good to those who love God and are called according to His purpose" (Romans 8:28). Don't be frustrated if an answer the Lord gave you doesn't materialize in the way you thought it would. For example, the answer to my prayer that I should sell one of my Web sites still hasn't led to the sale of that site, but it has led to many mini-sales from memberships on that Web site. The research I did in attempting to sell the site helped me find opportunities to earn the money I needed from the site by keeping it. The Lord pointed me in a direction that I could understand and that would give me hope and then once I marched in that direction, He opened up auxiliary doors of opportunity.

Pay Your Tithing. Solomon taught his son, "Honor the Lord with thy substance, and with the firstfruits of all thine increase: So shall thy barns be filled with plenty, and thy presses shall burst out with new wine" (Proverbs 3:9-10). No matter how little you have, show the Lord that you put Him first and that you are willing to do what He wants you to do by paying an honest tithe. Then the Lord will "open you the windows of heaven and pour you out a blessing that there shall not be room enough to receive it" (Malachi 3:10).

Fast. Isaiah taught that fasting and prayer could loose the bands of wickedness, undo heavy burdens, bring understanding and insight, increase health, bring prosperity and repair broken relationships. Through fasting and prayer, when you call, the Lord will answer, "Here I am" (Isaiah 58:5-12). A typical fast is to do without food and water for two consecutive meals or 24 hours. During that time you pray and meditate upon a desire or need you have for yourself or for others. Those with health concerns may adapt the fast to their circumstances. It is also customary, as explained in Isaiah to bless the poor and the needy by taking the money you saved from the missed meals and giving it to the poor.

Worship in the Lord's house. In the Lord's house we can receive timely instruction and inspiration. David put it so eloquently: "How amiable are thy tabernacles, O LORD of hosts! My soul longeth, yea, even fainteth for the courts of the Lord: my heart and my flesh crieth out for the living God. Blessed are they that dwell in thy house: they will be still praising thee. For a day in thy courts is better than a thousand. I had rather be a doorkeeper in the house of my God, than to dwell in the tents of wickedness. For the Lord God is a sun and shield: the Lord will give grace and glory: no good thing will he withhold from them that walk uprightly. O Lord of hosts, blessed is the man that trusteth in thee." (Psalms 84: 1-2, 4, 10-12)

Look for the lesson. Ask yourself what you can learn from this experience. What will you consider or do now that you might not have been willing or able to if you hadn't been called to endure this problem? How can you more empathetically help others? Squeeze lemonade from every lemon.

Reach out to others. Forget yourself and get lost in serving others. In the process you will find joy, happiness and a perspective on your own challenges that cannot be found in any other way than in selfless service to others.

I testify to you that these tools work. Even though challenges are not always removed immediately, God will give you the strength to endure them and peace to pass the time while they last.

For This Shall Give Thee Experience
by Mikalah Rennells

The heavens gather blackness
My soul in deep despair
Reaches upward outward
I know that He is there.

Fierce winds become my enemy
I cannot think or dare to be
Still onward ever onward
I strive on bended knee.

Alas the elements have combined
To hedge up my way and
My feet are shackled to the earth
But my heart can feel the spirit's sway.

The very jaws of hell gape
Open it's mouth wide after me
While standing on the edge afraid... then
He reaches down and sets me free!

I don't want to face trials
But somehow I should
For these shall be for
My experience and my good.

Chapter 2
Is This Treasure On Your List?

"If ye abide in me, and my words abide in you, ye shall ask what ye will, and it shall be done unto you."
- John 15: 7

Analyze the Desires of Your Heart

A desire is evidence of the power to accomplish that desire. Righteous desires are the results you seek in embryo. They are God seeking expression in your life. God is not cruel. If He plants a righteous desire in your heart, He prepares a way for you to accomplish the thing you desire. It may take time and the acquisition of wisdom and knowledge, but God-given desires are meant to come to fruition.

Where we most frequently trip up is misreading our desires. It's important to clearly define your desires. What is at the root of them? For example, the longing for a boyfriend or mate may really be the desire to be loved unconditionally. It may be that you are lonely and need companionship. The answer God gives may not be a husband, wife, boyfriend or girlfriend. It may be the companionship of the Spirit and an accompanying awareness of the unconditional love of the Savior for you. His answer may be a bounty of faithful friends or a church family. Realizing the root of your desires frees you to see the Lord's perfect solutions and to be grateful for them. If you tie the Lord into a specific way of delivering the fulfillment of your desires, you may blind yourself to a multitude of opportunities and rich blessings.

I remember a time when I was very lonely. My best friend had moved away and although I had other friends, I felt very alone because this one friend - who knew me better than anyone else - was no longer a daily part of my life. For several months I couldn't shake the feeling that there was a piece of me that could no longer find expression. I'm sure you've experienced that feeling – there are some people who you can talk to about anything – who understand everything about all the levels of who you are. When that person is pulled out of your life, it leaves a void. I thought the only solution was for the Lord to bring that friend back into my life, but instead He blessed me with four wonderful friends who together filled the void. Not only did they give me the companionship I needed at multiple levels, but they also brought me the next lessons that the Lord had for me to learn. Had there not been a void, there could never have been room for these other people to step in and touch my life.

I am grateful that the Lord has taught me to look deeper than the solution I think I need and to see the root of my desires. My desire represented a need for communication. It wasn't really a need for this one person. While that friendship will last forever, it was not what the Lord had in mind to fill my need to communicate. The Lord wanted me to do more than communicate; He wanted me to learn something new! That required the formation of closer relationships with existing friends and bringing new people into my life.

There are two things I've found that my Heavenly Father delights to give me -

understanding or knowledge and friends. Usually they come together in pairs. Invariably when a heavy question is weighing on my mind or I face a challenging situation, if I turn to the Lord in prayer for direction, in His perfect timing the answer comes. Usually a friend delivers the answer. Either the Lord will inspire someone I know to say or do something that addresses my need, or He will lead someone totally new into my life who has the answer to my question. What's even more beautiful is that I usually have the solution they need as well. God brings people together who have what each other needs. To watch Him work is a magnificent, awe-inspiring experience.

For example, one of the four friends I spoke of earlier opened up a wealth of practical knowledge that I began using to solve our family's financial crisis. Many of the principles which she taught me and which I began putting into practice are interlaced within this book. On her side of the situation, she needed help launching an online business, and I was able to help her in Web development and promotion. A second of these friends has been a big part of my life since 1995.

We started out as business partners, eventually dissolved that business, remained friends, but pursued separate interests. The Lord brought us full circle – working together again to not only solve both of our financial situations but also help some of our fellow Webmasters who have been struggling in a difficult Internet environment. Again, the economy of the Lord never ceases to amaze me – how He can answer so many people's prayers through His simple, strategic introductions.

What are the desires of your heart? What is at the root of them? Is it a need for companionship? Communication? To be heard? To be valued and loved? To make a difference in the world around you? Give those root desires to God and stand back and watch Him fulfill them in ways you never imagined. Don't try to control or manipulate the outcome or force relationships or events that are not part of His plan for you. Whether they seem inherently moral or right – they may not be your solution. Solutions are as unique as individuals, and the Lord is always full of pleasant surprises. Open yourself up to others.

You never know who holds your solution, and you may be the answer to their prayers.

Who Is That Blocking Your Path?

My dad has observed that even an earthworm will only bang its head against a rock about 20 times before it finally realizes it needs to go around the rock. So why are we human beings often less intelligent than an earthworm? When will we learn that if we keep on doing what we're doing, we'll keep on getting what we're getting? Sometimes that's a good thing. If we keep on praying and studying the Word of God, we'll keep on receiving inspiration. If we let those things slide, we won't.

But other times, we keep on doing things that don't yield results and expect that the next time somehow it's going to be different. There is a story in Numbers 22-24 that illustrates this point. It's about Balak, the king of the Moabites, and Balaam a Midianite prophet who served the Lord. Balak saw the hosts of Israelites flooding the land, destroying the wicked cities and he was scared they'd come after the Moabites. He sent his servants to the prophet Balaam to ask him to return with them and curse the Israelites. Balaam prayed to the Lord, but the Lord said, "Thou shalt not go with them; thou shalt not curse the people: for they are blessed." So Balaam told the men that he couldn't go curse the people. The messengers returned to Balak with this report.

Balak wouldn't take no for an answer, so he sent more men to fetch Balaam and promise him great honor and whatever he asked if he would come curse the Israelites. Balaam replied to them, "If Balak would give me his house full of silver and gold, I cannot go beyond the word of the LORD my God, to do less or more." But, he asked the men to stay in the area for the night and he'd ask the Lord one more time. The Lord replied, "If the men come to call thee, rise up, and go with them; but yet the word which I shall say unto thee, that shalt thou do."

The next morning, Balaam got up, saddled his donkey and went with the princes of Moab. But the Bible says that "God's anger was kindled because he went: and the angel of the Lord stood in the way for an adversary against him." Didn't the Lord tell him he should go, but just to say what he was told to say? So why was the Lord angry? Evidently, Balaam had some other ideas in his heart. Maybe he was thinking about the honor and riches he would receive if he cursed the people as Balak requested. The donkey on which Balaam was riding saw the angel of the Lord with his sword drawn in his hand, so the donkey turned off into the field. Balaam smote the donkey to turn her back onto the road. But a little bit further down the road, the angel stood in the path again. There was a wall on the left and the right, so when the donkey saw the angel of the Lord, she thrust herself against the wall and crushed Balaam's foot. He smote her again. The angel went further and stood in a narrow place where there was no way to turn either to the right hand or to the left. And when the donkey saw the angel, she fell down under Balaam and Balaam was so angry he started beating her with a staff.

Notice how the Lord keeps narrowing the options to help Balaam get the message. But he still doesn't get the hint so the Lord opened the donkey's mouth and she said to Balaam, "What have I done unto thee that thou hast smitten me these three times? Balaam told the donkey, "Because thou hast mocked me: I would there were a sword in mine hand, for now would I kill thee." The donkey replied, "Am not I thy donkey, upon which thou hast ridden ever since I was thine unto this day? Was I ever wont to do so unto thee?" And he said, "Nay." Balaam is still pretty dense; after all he's carrying on a conversation with a donkey!

Then the Lord opened Balaam's eyes so he could see the angel standing in the way, and his sword drawn in his hand. Balaam bowed down his head, and fell flat on his face. The angel of the Lord said, "Wherefore hast thou smitten thine donkey these three times? Behold, I went out to withstand thee, because thy way is perverse before me: and the donkey saw me, and turned from me these three times: unless she had turned from me, surely now also I had slain thee, and saved her alive."

Balaam said to the angel, "I have sinned; for I knew not that thou stoodest in the way against me: now therefore, if it displease thee, I will get me back again." The angel replied, "Go with the men: but only the word that I shall speak unto thee that thou shalt speak." So Balaam went with the princes of Balak.

When Balaam arrives, Balak takes him to a high place to show him the Israelites swarming the land. He asks Balaam to build 7 altars and sacrifice 7 oxen and 7 rams on them and curse the Israelites. Balaam makes the sacrifices and asks the Lord, but the Lord doesn't curse the Israelites, He blesses them. Balak takes Balaam to a second and a third location to view the people and builds the same number of altars and sacrifices on each of them. But each time Balaam offers more and more blessings upon the Israelites and prophecies of the destruction of the existing people in the land. Finally, Balak sends him away.

Notice how many times Balaam and Balak had to be given a message before they'd get it through their thick heads that God wasn't going to let them curse the Israelites. Are we that hard headed sometimes? Do we keep pursuing paths even when God is blocking our efforts on every side? Granted, the adversary can also work to thwart our efforts and we must not misinterpret his advances as God telling us to quit. But we can run our situation down a bit of a checklist:

Is what you want to do something that is against God's will? Is it written in the scriptures as something you should or shouldn't be doing?

Is your heart right? Are you pursuing this course for your own honor or glory?

Did you receive an initial answer from the Lord? Are you staying true to God's initial message or are you working and reworking the situation to serve your own purposes? No matter how many times they asked, how many sacrifices they were willing to make or how many places they asked from, the Lord's answer didn't change.

If we are heading down the path the Lord directed and we're going with an eye single to His glory but we still meet with opposition, it most likely is the adversary's attempts to keep us from going forward. It is important to distinguish the difference between Satan's attempts to keep us from doing what God wants and God telling us we're on the wrong path or pursuing with the wrong motives. That's why it's so important to study God's Word to know what His policies are, and also why it's so important to seek a solid answer when making important decisions.

Confirmation Is Key

The critical foundation under-girding any life that seeks to follow the will of God is a confirmation that your life is on course and that the path you are pursuing is the one God has in mind for you. Without that confirmation, there's nothing to build your faith upon. If you're not sure whether God wants something for you, how can you exercise faith to believe He will bring it to pass? You can't! The last thing you need to do is waste energy pursuing a path that is contrary to God's will for you.

Turn to the Word

How can you be certain you are on the right path? The first place to turn is the Word of God. "Search the scriptures, for in them ye think ye have eternal life and they are they which testify of me." (John 5:39). Ask yourself if the desire of your heart or the path you are following is in accordance with the established commandments of God. If you are violating God's commands, then it's obvious your path is faulty. The first order of business is to get your life back in harmony with God's laws. Once you've done that, you'll be prepared to hear the voice of the Lord for custom direction especially for you.

Sometimes we pray for things that we already know the answer to. Within the scriptures are advice and direction in the way that we should live. Have you searched the scriptures for your answer? For example, if you are struggling with whether you should forgive a person who has seriously offended you, and you pray to the Lord for guidance in this, you may feel you aren't getting an answer. But in reality, the answer has already been given to you. It is found in the scriptures. (See Matthew 18:21-35)

It's human nature to think that we're the exception to the rule. "Sure, I know the scriptures teach that, but my case is different. I need the Lord to tell me specifically what to do in my situation." But the truth is you and I are not the exceptions. We need to be willing to act upon the Lord's commands first. Then, as we act, we will feel a confirmation that our decision is the right one. We will have feelings of peace and contentment that following the Lord's commandments is truly the best course for us. But, it is up to us to act *before* we get an answer in such cases. Jesus said, "If any man will do his will, he shall know of the doctrine, whether it be of God, or whether I speak of myself." (John 7:17)

Aside from matters of right and wrong, there are many reassuring promises to be found in the scriptures. The Lord definitely has a desire for the healing of marriages, the removal of His people from bondage and the salvation of souls, etc. Search the scriptures and if you find precedence for the blessing you seek then you can claim that scripture when you present your petition to the Lord. You will be in a better position to trust and know that the desire of your heart is in accordance with His will. The promised blessing may not be immediate – the Lord's timing is rarely our timing, but if you obey the laws, you can claim the promises.

Relax and Be Patient

Often when our need is most desperate, answers seem slowest in coming. Have you ever been in a hurry to get out the door but can't find your keys? You're desperate — you search everywhere with no luck. Then you decide to sit for a minute and calm down and think. You get up and there your keys are, in an obvious location that you may have even searched before.

Similarly, in our frantic state, we are often too stressed to open our spiritual eyes and see answers that are in plain view. Sometimes our cries for help drown out the still small voice that is speaking the answers.

Relax. Try to emotionally detach yourself from the situation, look at it objectively, find a quiet place to pray and really listen for answers.

He Never Promised A "Yes"

Because the Lord has an eternal perspective of our existence, He knows best about what we need in our lives. Sometimes, in our own best interests, the Lord tells us "No" – even when we pray for something that seems like it should be perfectly acceptable to Him. It takes faith to believe that Heavenly Father knows best and that if He says "No" that that's still an answer, and it's one that will be best for us in the long run.

The Apostle Paul prayed three times that the thorn in his flesh would be removed. But the answer each time was "No." I have a feeling that

Paul probably spent three seasons of his life praying that this challenge be resolved, but he was left to endure it. Rather than be bitter or complain, Paul looked for the positive and realized that this "thorn in his flesh" kept him humble. It made him see His human weakness so that He could more readily glory in the grace of God that strengthened him to endure his trial (2 Corinthians 12).

He Never Promised "When"

The Lord often asks us to wait a while. His timing is always the best timing. Not only should we say, "Thy will be done" but we also need to learn to say, "Thy timing be done." I am reminded of a tough six years in our married life when my husband and I experienced serious financial challenges. The answer to our prayers was not that we would be immediately delivered from our financial situation, instead we were given hope, peace and the ability to endure it as we worked to correct the situation. The Lord often wants us to work through serious challenges so that we can grow in wisdom and faith. In such cases, I have found it helpful to ask, "What can I learn from this situation? What do I know now and how am I a better person for having endured this hardship?" I have found that the lessons learned are always worth the price paid.

He Will Not Force the Agency of Others

While we may have faith in the Lord and what He would like to have happen, we can't always count on other people to use their free will (agency) to choose what the Lord wants. When our prayers involve the choices of others, we must be especially patient. The Lord will never force anyone to see the light or to choose His will in answer to your prayers. He may gently persuade, lead and guide them until they eventually see the light, but He will not force Himself upon them. Patience is critical when our prayers involve the agency of others.

The best advice I can give about situations that involve the poor choices of others is to pray that the other person's heart may be softened and that s/he may be led to the Lord. In the meantime prayerfully consult the Lord about all the ways you can lovingly and patiently serve the person until the time comes that his/her heart is softened. When we are anxious and earnest about the salvation of others, the Lord may choose to reveal to us a vision of their eventual salvation, that we might have the hope and faith to lovingly lead them to the light. But remember that your role is simply to lead, never to push, coerce, manipulate or force. No one ever drove anyone into the Kingdom of Heaven with a club. That's not the way the Lord wants it done, and quite frankly, it won't work because salvation is a personal choice.

I've made more than my share of mistakes in this department. I've used plenty of Satan's tactics all in the name of "saving souls." As my favorite math teacher was fond of saying, "The end never justifies the means." Satan's tactics include impatience, coercion, manipulation, guilt tripping, sarcasm and force. None of these should be a part of the Christian's toolbox – especially not when trying to help someone onto the right path. While the Lord may use our efforts to bring about His purposes, it is pride and arrogance on our part to think He can't accomplish His ends without us. Meddling into His plan or timetable for another person's life is unrighteous dominion – even if we think we're doing it "for their own good."

Did You Hear That Answer?

Moses heard the Lord's voice from a burning bush. Joseph dreamed dreams. Saul (later Paul) saw a vision, but rarely do we hear voices, see visions or dream dreams. Instead, we may have strokes of ideas or inspiration come into our minds. We may be reading a verse of scripture and it may trigger ideas for what we should do next. We may be speaking with a friend and she may have the answer we seek. Still other times we may experience a feeling of peace and comfort that lets us know what we should do. It is important to learn to listen and recognize answers and not to dismiss them as simply coincidence or our own voice within our head.

There are other factors that can play a role in whether our prayers are being answered, but they are always on our end of the communication channel. The Lord always listens. It is up to us to keep the channels clean by being obedient to the Lord, listening, learning to recognize His voice, and being willing to accept His will instead of our own.

If you aren't sure whether the answers you're receiving are from God or are just in your own head, begin praying for the Lord to teach you what it feels like and sounds like to receive an answer from Him. Search the scriptures to learn how God communicates with His children, and prayerfully seek His direction in learning to recognize His voice. Gradually you will learn the language of the Spirit – the language of personal revelation - just as you would learn any other language.

Chapter 3
Faith: The Stuff From Which Treasures Are Made

"Faith is the substance of things hoped for, the evidence of things not seen" - Hebrews 11:1.

Think of faith as the modeling clay (the substance) from which God builds miracles. If you need healing in your marriage, faith is the substance from which God will rebuild your marriage. If you need physical healing, a new car, a roof over your head, your debts paid off, a believing spouse, whatever you need, God will build the answer to your prayer from your faith. Your faith is the literal substance from which God constructs your miracle. If it's not there, nothing gets built.

In John chapter 9 there is an account of a man who was born blind whom Jesus healed in an unusual way. Normally Jesus healed people with a word or a touch but in this man's case He spit on the ground, made clay from the spittle and put the clay on the man's eyes. He then told the man to go wash himself in a pool and he would see. While this account is rich with symbolism about spiritual blindness and even baptism there is a message about faith here as well.

Think of the clay that Jesus used as a symbol for faith – the substance of the miracle. This clay or working faith was comprised of the dust of the ground and water from Jesus' mouth. The dust of the ground represents our faith – our part of the formula. The spit represents the living waters that Jesus provides – His enabling grace that empowers our faith. While our faith is necessary and critical, it alone won't "stick" to the problems or challenges of our lives. It won't heal spiritual or physical blindness. It alone won't heal broken lives, homes or bodies. But together with Christ's living water miracles occur.

This is why it is so important to make sure that what you are seeking is in accordance with God's will. No amount of faith will do the trick if what you have faith in is false or in violation of God's will for you. The priests of Baal had faith in their god, but no amount of faith in that false god could bring down fire from heaven (1 Kings 18). You need Christ's part of the formula to make your goal a successful reality. He will only lend His enabling grace to an outcome for which He approves. Granted, on occasion, your faith alone may lead to the outcome you seek, but if it is not in accordance with God's will, it will be a hollow victory.

Notice that Jesus applied the clay to the blind man's eyes for him. He didn't hand it to the blind man and tell him to put it on his own eyes. Jesus is the Master Healer. He takes the mixture of our faith and His power, applies it to broken lives, hearts, dreams and relationships and heals them. Of course, the blind man was a willing participant in this. He allowed Jesus to heal Him. He exercised his faith to walk to the pool and wash the clay from his eyes. He put forth some effort. As James 2:20 says, "faith without works is dead."

I have a feeling that after Jesus healed this man in such an unconventional way, His disciples queried him later, "Lord, why did you use clay to heal this man's blindness? We've never seen you do that before." Jesus may have said something like, "Just as the clay was applied to this man that he might see, so faith and the power of God combined heals anything that is broken. Grace-enabled faith is the substance of things hoped for - the evidence of things not seen. The things which are impossible with men are possible with God" (Luke 18:27).

Faith is critical in defining what we control and what God controls. What part did this blind man control and what role did Christ play? The only part the blind man really controlled was whether He would allow Christ to apply the clay and whether he would follow instructions. That was it. God did the rest. In your life, that's the extent of what God asks you to do to make all things work together for your good. First you invite Him into the situation by requesting His help, you have faith and expect that He will, and then you follow any instructions He gives you.

You don't take it upon yourself to add more or take away from His instructions. You do simply what the Lord directs you to do – just as the blind man did as he was directed and washed in the pool.⁴

So what are you directed to do? There are the standard things we are all commanded to do – such as loving our neighbors as ourselves and loving the Lord our God with all our might, mind and strength. Those commandments are the same for everyone, but when your situation does not directly involve right and wrong, the Lord's directions may vary. For example, leprous Naman in the Old Testament was to wash himself seven times in the River Jordan. The blind man in our story washed his eyes in a nearby pool. For a lame man, Christ's directive was "arise, take up thy bed and walk." The solution for the woman with an issue of blood for 12 years was to simply touch the hem of His garment. While principles are universal, the application of those principles may vary from person to person.

Truth is universal, timeless and unchanging, but the solutions for two righteous individuals could be very different. That is where the need for personal revelation comes in. The Holy Spirit reveals to each individual the custom guidance he or she needs on a need to know basis. But one must be in tune with the Spirit to hear it and recognize its direction.

Vision Determines Your Destiny

Have you given up on your dreams? Have you resigned yourself to believing that God just must not want you to have them? Don't give up. God is ready and willing to help you achieve your worthy goals. If you aren't accomplishing them, don't blame God; the problem is more likely in yourself and how you're looking at life and your Heavenly Father. Father delights to give good gifts to his children (Matthew 7:11). But, we must learn to access His inspiration and guidance, and work within His laws to make our worthy dreams a reality.

Looking back on my life, I've noticed that every significant accomplishment began with a picture in my mind of the end result. If I can't picture myself accomplishing a goal or task, then I won't do it. Not until I can get an emotionally charged mental picture of myself achieving something, am I able to do it. To achieve any worthy goal, we must first have a purpose for accomplishing it, a desire to do so, and a vision of the end result. Proverbs 29:18 tells us, "Where there is no vision, the people perish: but he that keepeth the law, happy is he." Vision is critical to accomplishing any goal or objective. Matter of fact, without it we (and our dreams) "perish."

Proverbs 23:7 says, "For as he thinketh in his heart, so is he." The thoughts we hold in our hearts (those we hold with emotion – they're in our hearts, not just our heads) determine who we are and what we become. If we think negative thoughts or visualize worrisome outcomes for our future, then our emotionally charged negative vision becomes a self-fulfilling prophecy. Job, the great sufferer of the Bible, lamented, "For the thing which I greatly feared is come upon me, and that which I was afraid of is come unto me." (Job 3:25) Fear often becomes a self-fulfilling prophecy. But if we think positive thoughts and hold a positive vision for our future, then those thoughts direct our paths.

When we prayerfully seek the Lord's path for our lives, and begin to understand His will for us, it is critical to hold a positive vision of ourselves achieving what we know the Lord wants for us. For example, if you are in excessive debt, you can turn to scripture and see that the Lord does not wish you to be. For "the borrower is a servant to the lender" (Proverbs 22:7). It is God's will that you be debt-free. So, instead of imagining all the worse case scenarios or visualizing yourself going into bankruptcy, visualize what you want. Instead of spending your time worrying, visualize what your life would look like and feel like if you were completely debt free. Prayerfully hold that vision in your mind, with faith, believing that the Lord will give it to you, because it is His will that you be free.

As you spend time each day visualizing the outcome you want, offer prayers of heartfelt gratitude to your Father in Heaven for the deliverance that is on its way to you. Within a short time of holding this image in your daily thoughts, you will begin to receive insights into things you can do or people you can talk to who will help you reach your goal. Immediately follow any prompting from the Spirit as you prayerfully visualize your desired outcome. No matter how small or insignificant it may be, immediately follow through on the impulses and ideas that come to you. Here's an example of how listening to the still small voice can make a drastic difference in your life.

> After returning from Florida in June, my husband and I decided to fast and pray about our financial situation. The answer received was a simple one. "It will be according to your faith. Expect a miracle." A couple of months passed and each day I mustered my resolve and strength to "have faith and expect a miracle." We began prospering by degrees, struggling, but meeting

obligations. Occasionally I would find myself taking the load back upon my own shoulders. Then I'd realize what I'd done and consciously give it back to the Lord through prayer and placing our family budget behind the picture of Christ on my desk. It was a daily struggle to give the problem to the Lord.

In August, I began praying, "Lord, you know how to make my business grow so that we can fix this problem. Please teach me what I need to know to increase my business and pay off this debt."

A couple weeks later, I was preparing my weekly SheLovesGod article. Each week before I write these articles, I kneel and ask the Lord to give me the message that He wants the people on the list to have. Invariably, He gives me a topic and the words. At this particular time in my life I was doing a lot of research on forgiveness. I was struggling off and on to forgive someone who had been instrumental in our current predicament. The answer was clear that I should write that week's article on forgiveness.

Shortly after the article was posted on the site, I received an email from a lady named Leslie. She wrote me to say that she was struggling with forgiving someone. Normally she is a very forgiving person, but this was just a very difficult situation for her. She asked if she could share her story and get my thoughts on the matter. I agreed, and she sent me her story. It was a complicated predicament and I could understand why she was struggling with forgiveness.

After reading her story, I felt as though I must share mine. But I hesitated. I really didn't want to share my private life with a total stranger. But she had been so open and honest. I felt I owed her an answer. I prayed about it and felt that I should be open with her and share my struggle with forgiveness.

When Leslie realized that my troubles were financial she basically said, "Oh, now *that* I can help you with. I have learned some principles or laws that govern abundant living that I would be happy to share with you."

And that was the beginning. Leslie began teaching me the laws of abundant living. As I learned them, I was amazed at the new level of faith that I had in the Lord. All the randomness of life melted away and I could see how the Lord works in our lives. He truly gives us what we expect in our hearts. To be honest, my husband and I never really "expected" to prosper. We saw ourselves as "just getting by." We didn't think prosperous thoughts, and thus we got what we expected. (More on this in Chapter 6.)

The information I learned from Leslie allowed me to totally forgive because one of the laws states that within every bad situation is an equal and opposite good. If something is a little bad, then there is a little good laced within it. If it is catastrophic, then there is something phenomenal within it. I began to look for the good within our situation and realized that had we never come to this financial crisis, I never would have learned the life-changing, faith-increasing principles that Leslie shared with me*. As a matter of fact, I never even would have met Leslie, who has become a dear friend to me. For me, the sacrifice was merely an investment in something totally priceless. It took me from struggling day-by-day to muster faith, to a constant abiding faith – a peace that passes all understanding.

I am so grateful that the Spirit prompted me to write that article on forgiveness and that He prompted me to be honest and open with a stranger.

Don't beat yourself up over past mistakes. Let the past go and concentrate on holding a picture in your mind of the outcome you want. Live in the now. Yesterday is gone, the future isn't here yet, so take advantage of today. Act

---

* For more information on Leslie Householder and what she teaches, visit www.ThoughtsAlive.com

immediately on the direction the Lord gives you for today.

Be patient. Every seed must be planted and be given time to grow before the harvest can come. But rest assured, if you hold your vision with purpose and faith, and act when prompted, the results the Lord has in store for you will come to pass. Habakkuk 2:3-4 assures us, "For the vision is yet for an appointed time, but at the end it shall speak, and not lie: though it tarry, wait for it; because it will surely come, it will not tarry…the just shall live by his faith."

Whenever you are tempted to give up or think all is lost, concentrate on the vision of your outcome. Let the light of vision dispel the darkness of doubt, fear or worry. Gratefully thank the Lord for the things you already have and the things that are coming to you. Gratitude is the illuminating catalyst that turns your vision of faith into a reality. Romans 1:21 warns that an unthankful heart is one that is foolish and darkened. In contrast, a thankful heart is filled with the illumination of the Spirit of the Lord that will guide your steps.

Seek to learn and live God's laws, for as the second half of Proverbs 29:18 says, "he that keepeth the law, happy is he." When we keep the commandments and abide within the laws of God, we have His Spirit to be with us. The Spirit then guides us in wise decisions that will lead us to happiness, freedom and peace. Seek the Spirit of the Lord; pray for it in your life. Hold the vision of your outcome and it will give you the desire, the patience and the faith to do whatever is necessary to make your goal a reality. "Delight thyself in the Lord; and He shall give thee the desires of thine heart" (Psalm 37:4).

As the Lord reveals to you a vision of your outcome, write it down. Writing a clear description of your vision raises it from simply a wish to a goal. The more detailed the written description of your goal, the more likely it will be achieved – that's a proven fact.

Chapter 4
Gratitude: The Key That Unlocks the Treasury of Heaven

"Praise the Lord; for his mercy endureth forever"
- 2 Chronicles 20:21

There's an old Jewish (Hasidic) story that tells of a man who met two of his friends while traveling down a road. He asked the two men how things were going in their lives. The first friend answered that things were horrible. He declared that he'd be better off dead. Life was hard and nothing seemed to be going his way. God, hearing their conversation from heaven commented, "You think you've got it bad now, you ungrateful man, you haven't seen anything yet!"

The second friend answered, "Life is wonderful! God is good. Everything is coming up roses. I am so incredibly blessed!" God, hearing this reply from heaven answered, "What a delightfully grateful soul! You think you've got it good now, just wait and see what wonderful things await you!"

The Lord delights to bless those with a grateful heart. Colossians 3:17 gives the secret for making the best of your life: "And whatsoever ye do in word or deed, do all in the name of the Lord Jesus, giving thanks to God and the Father by Him."

Think about that! What if everything you did, you did in the name of the Lord and gave thanks to God in His name! We'd all get into a lot less trouble if we followed this advice wouldn't we? Imagine the good we could do in the world if we took the time to put our best efforts into every task – knowing that we wanted the Lord Jesus Christ to lend His name and approval to our every action!

James 4:8 teaches "Draw nigh to God, and He will draw nigh to you." We draw nigh to God by living His teachings, by seeking to do what He would have us do, and by showing a grateful heart. No matter how bad life gets, we can always find something for which to be grateful. Even in our times of trouble, we can be thankful knowing that this too shall pass and the sun will come out tomorrow.

The surest way to bring yourself into harmony with God and put yourself into a position to receive blessings and directions at His hand is through a sense of deep and profound gratitude. Gratitude brings you into harmony with the mind and will of God. It draws you nigh to Him and He in turn will be drawn to you. Think of it from your own human perspective. Who are you drawn to more – a person who is ungrateful and demanding or someone who shows genuine gratitude for what you have done for them? How does a person's gratitude affect what you will do for them in the future?

I remember a time a friend and I gathered in prayer to petition the Lord for a mutual friend's father who was about to undergo extensive surgery. My friend offered the prayer and if anyone could reach up, touch heaven and gain audience with the ear of the Almighty, my friend could do it. She started by acknowledging the greatness of our Father and the matchless mercy available to us through His Son Jesus Christ. Then she began thanking the Lord for the miracle that He was about to work in the life of this man. She painted a picture of the surgeon leaving the operating room with the good news that all went well and that the surgery was a success. In humble gratitude she thanked the Lord **before** the event took place and painted a vivid picture of the events as they would unfold. I felt as if I were there, her words were so vivid.

Upon the final Amen, I knew within my heart that Heavenly Father would do anything and everything within His power to see that His daughter's prayer was answered to the smallest detail. Any loving Father would delight to honor and fulfill the prayer of such a grateful and honest heart. The only thing that would stop it is if He had other plans that simply must come to pass.

1 Chronicles 29:11-1 contains a wonderful truth:

> "Thine, O LORD, is the greatness, and the power, and the glory, and the victory, and the majesty: for all that is in the heaven and in the earth is thine; thine is the kingdom, O LORD, and thou art exalted as head above all.

> "Both riches and honour come of thee, and thou reignest over all; and in thine hand is power and might; and in thine hand it is to make great, and to give strength unto all. Now therefore, our God, we thank thee, and praise thy glorious name."

The truth is, that if we want to receive blessings from the Lord – whether physical, mental or spiritual, the first step is to show genuine gratitude for the things we already have and for the things we hope to receive in the future. It makes only logical sense that the closer we live to God (from whom all riches flow), the more we will receive of those riches. "For it is your Father's good pleasure to give you the kingdom." (Luke 12: 32) and we draw nigh to the Father through intense gratitude, grounded in His Son Jesus Christ. If all you had to be grateful for was the gift of His Son, then that would be more than enough! Ponder on that fact for a moment!

Jesus, our great Exemplar, showed gratitude in all things. Before he fed the multitudes with the meager loaves and fishes, He gave thanks to His Father. Before He raised Lazarus from the dead, he said, "Father I thank thee that thou hast heard me." (John 11:41) He even found something to be grateful for when people rejected His message. "Jesus rejoiced in spirit, and said, I thank thee, O Father, Lord of heaven and earth, that thou hast hid these things from the wise and prudent, and hast revealed them unto babes." (Luke 10: 21)

Start today and think of ways that you can show more gratitude to God for His blessings and even your challenges. Here are a few ideas to get you started. I'm sure you'll think of more.

- Spend as much time thanking the Lord for an answer to prayer as you spent pleading for Him to give it to you.

- Offer one prayer a day that is nothing but a prayer of gratitude. Don't ask for anything, don't complain, just thank Him!

- Keep a gratitude journal of things that you are grateful for and write in it every day. When you're disappointed, feel like giving up, or just need a lift go back and read this journal.

- When other people do things for you, thank them and thank the Lord for bringing them into your life.

- While you're doing automatic tasks that don't require your higher mental faculties (like washing dishes, mowing the lawn, etc.) count your blessings. List them in your mind.

- Thank the Lord in advance for the things you know He'll do for you in the future.

- In any difficult situation, look for the good. Laced within every negative event is an equal and opposite good. You will find it if you thankfully look for it!

"Give thanks always for all things unto God and the Father in the name of our Lord Jesus Christ"
- Ephesians 5:20

Practice Worshipful Waiting

There's a delightful story found in 2 Chronicles 20 that is froth with lessons in overcoming major life challenges. Jehoshaphat, the fourth great grandson of Solomon was king of Judah. He was a good, honorable man who served the Lord – a novelty among a long line of wicked kings. When the Israelites first entered the Promised Land, the Lord instructed them to leave the Moabites and the Ammonites alone because they had their own portions of the Promised Land. But by the time Jehoshaphat came to power, the Moabites and Ammonites were corrupt and prepared to make war against Judah.

Jehoshaphat feared because his people were greatly outnumbered, but he didn't let fear get the better of him. He turned to the Lord, gathered his people together and proclaimed a fast throughout all Judah (2 Chronicles 20:3). He cried to the Lord, "we have no might against this great company that cometh against us; neither know we what to do; but our eyes are upon thee." And all of Judah stood before the Lord, with their little ones, their wives, and their children (2 Chronicles 20:12-13).

Then the Lord spoke to the people through the prophet Jahaziel, "Be not afraid nor dismayed by reason of this great multitude; for the battle is not yours, but God's. Tomorrow go ye down against them… Ye shall not need to fight in this battle: set yourselves, stand ye still, and see the salvation of the Lord with you, O Judah and Jerusalem: fear not, nor be dismayed; tomorrow go out against them: for the Lord will be with you" (2 Chronicles 20:16-17).

Jehoshaphat and all of Judah bowed themselves before the Lord and worshipped Him. The Levite priests praised the Lord with a loud voice. Jehoshaphat stood before the people and said, "Hear me, O Judah, and ye inhabitants of

Jerusalem; Believe in the Lord your God, so shall ye be established; believe his prophets, so shall ye prosper" (2 Chronicles 20:19-20).

Then Jehoshaphat appointed singers who went before the army and praised the Lord through song, "Praise the Lord; for his mercy endureth forever" (2 Chronicles 20:21). And then the children of Ammon, Moab and Mount Seir began to fight one another and destroyed each other and none escaped. It took Jehoshaphat and his people three days to gather up and carry away the riches that were left by their enemies. They continued to praise the Lord for His miraculous deliverance.

This story gives 10 tools for obtaining deliverance from insurmountable challenges.

- **Pray to the Lord for help.** Jehoshaphat and the people turned to the true and living God. They didn't turn to idols that their ancestors worshipped. They knew the one true God and only Him did they serve.

- **Fast with others.** Jehoshaphat proclaimed a fast throughout the entire kingdom. He knew that when faithful followers of God fast and pray together, there is increased efficacy in drawing upon the powers of heaven.

- **Gather together with others**. The people of Judah gathered together, prayed together and strengthened one another. In our times of trial, we can draw strength from other believers who will help us stay strong and faithful.

- **Acknowledge your own inability to solve the problem**. Jehoshaphat acknowledged to the Lord that he and his people were outnumbered, that they had no clue how to proceed, and that they could not face this enemy alone. They needed God.

- **Keep your eyes on the Lord**. When acknowledging that he didn't know what to do and didn't have the ability to defeat the enemy, Jehoshaphat added, "but our eyes are upon thee." When our eyes are fixed on the

Lord, we gain the faith and strength to carry us through.

- **Stand still and expect the salvation of the Lord.** Although many times we must work to free ourselves from difficult situations, in this instance, the people of Judah were told that the battle was not theirs, but was God's. They were to be still and wait faithfully for their deliverance. When the Lord has made a promise to deliver us, we can stay focused by being still and waiting for Him to show His hand.

- **Have faith, not fear.** The Lord and Jehoshaphat told the people not to be afraid. Fear and doubt cast out faith. It's important not to allow these tools of the adversary to encroach upon the stage of your mind. Cast them out swiftly by fixing your eyes on the Lord.

- **Believe God's prophets.** Jehoshaphat reminded the people to listen to the guidance the Lord had revealed to them through His prophets.

- **Praise the Lord before the problem is solved**. The people praised the Lord through words and song before they ever received their solution. They trusted the Lord that He would keep His word and praised Him as if their deliverance had already come. They also made sure to continue praising Him afterward.

- **Worship the Lord through music**. Rather than send forth men to fight, Jehoshaphat sent forth singers to praise the Lord. Inspirational, praise music has a way of keeping us focused on the Lord and builds our trust in Him.

Even when we know the Lord will ultimately deliver us, I think it's human nature to feel the need to take control of the situation and manufacture our own solutions – to speed up the process. But, to their credit, these people didn't do that. They didn't try to second guess the Lord or predict how He would deliver them. They just trusted that He would. They believed the Lord when He said they wouldn't have to fight and they spent their energies praising the Lord and worshipping Him through song. I find it admirable that although they didn't have a clue how their deliverance would come, they didn't jump in and try to form solutions. Although work is a good thing, I think sometimes I lean too much on my own ingenuity and not enough on the Lord's promises. Rather than muddying the waters with my forced solutions, often I think my time would be better spent praising through music and worshipfully waiting. How about you?

Chapter 5
Your Navigating Co-Pilot

"Trust in the Lord with all thine heart; and lean not upon thine own understanding. In all thy ways acknowledge Him and He shall direct thy paths."
- Proverbs 3:5-6

In our road trip analogy of life, one might think that you should turn over the vehicle to God and let Him drive. But, I don't believe God wants to drive your vehicle. I think He wants you to learn to drive it for yourself. He'll never ask you to relinquish your agency. He only asks you to use your free will to seek His input and follow His advice. He wants to be your Navigating Co-Pilot. He wants you to invite Him to sit next to you because He has the map and knows where all your treasures lie and the best routes for attaining them. You can either stumble through life blind, or you can ask God, who has the master map for your life, to be your Navigating Co-Pilot. The answer is obvious.

Why do I use the term Navigating Co-Pilot instead of just Navigator? Because there are times when life's hurdles become so insurmountable, that we need the Lord to take over the controls and pilot us through the situation. What good is a lifeguard who won't get wet? What good is a Savior who won't save? Jesus Christ isn't simply a wonderful Cheerleader or Coach, He's a Player on your team.

Some terrain's take supernatural pilot skills to maneuver. God is the champion of lost causes. Think of David and Goliath, Gideon with his 300 men, and Joshua at Jericho. There are points along your journey where the only way you can learn the required lesson and develop the next level of faith is to face a hurdle that is humanly impossible for you. At this point, most humans try everything they can and ultimately, generally in tear-filled humility, surrender the controls to the Lord. This is what He wants you to learn – how to trust in Him, to lean on Him. It's a humbling experience to realize that we can't control everything and that we need His grace to exist.

If you're driving your vehicle with God as your Navigating Co-Pilot, then you're searching the scriptures daily and praying several times a day or even better, "praying without ceasing" (1 Thessalonians 5:17). You're in tune with the Spirit of the Lord so that if He sends a message, you have ears to hear and eyes to see. It follows that if you are going to this trouble to live a life that is in tune with the Spirit of the Lord, that when you hear Him speak, you will follow instructions immediately. To do otherwise would be foolish. Disregarding a prompting from the Spirit is tantamount to not veering to miss an obstacle, or worse taking a wrong road, which may lead to dangerous paths.

True faith propels us to action. A faith that does not lead to action is not true faith. It is merely a wish. Your job is to hold onto your vision of faith and prayerfully follow every direction you receive from the Lord. That's the extent of your control of the situation. You can't control where other people drive their vehicles. You can't control rain or snow storms. You can't stop obstacles that fall across your path or drunk drivers that strike you from behind. All these things are just a part of life. God doesn't throw the boulder across your path. He doesn't cause the road to be slick with ice and snow. Nor does He cause other people who have refused Him as their Navigating Co-Pilot to crash into your path. All of these things are just part of life on earth. They're just hazards of the journey.

God controls the map, but His map is no ordinary map. It's a dynamic, prophetic aerial map that shows Him where future challenges lie. It's intricately interwoven into other people's journeys. He knows how your map intersects with others. He arranges rendezvous with other people so that you can help each other find what you need. "It is not good that man (or woman) should be alone" (Genesis 2:18). We need each other. Anyone who shuts others out, shuts out his or her own blessings.

While God will not interfere with the agency of others, He will help you find detours and ways to deal with the challenges that other people throw across your path. If He decides that you must wade through a challenge rather than circumvent it, then He is doing it for a reason. There is a treasure hidden within the quagmire. The greater the challenge, the greater the reward.

Knowing When to Act and When to Be Still

The most difficult decision most of us face is whether to act or be still and wait. When is it time to fight and when is it time to let the Lord fight your battles?

The answer is really very simple. All you have to do is trust your Heavenly Father and follow directions. Don't get out and push unless He tells you to. Don't take detours unless He directs. Don't forge ahead and insist on traversing dangerous paths, unless He instructs you to do so. If you don't know what to do, then do nothing. "Be Still and know that I am God," He says. In other words, when in doubt, don't. Stop and listen.

This advice makes sense in an abstract way, but it may be more difficult when you're in the middle of a crisis. Many times we feel the need to forge ahead in dogged determination to make something work. Granted, there are times when you should fight for what you want and never give up, but there are other times that your frantic fighting and clawing obliterates the voice of the Spirit that is trying to direct you.

A simple example of this is when I'm stumped with a programming problem. Occasionally in my business I am required to do some computer programming that taxes my abilities and knowledge. Usually I'm like a dog with a bone and refuse to give up until I figure it out. Several years ago, my husband taught me a little trick to use when I'm stumped. He told me "take a break and come back to it later." At first I refused to listen to him. After all, I was on a deadline. I didn't have time for a break and what did he know about programming anyway? I prayed for help on the problem, but the solution didn't come. Eventually, I relented to his advice, stepped away from the computer and did something else for a while. When I came back to it, voila, there was the answer – so simple and staring me right in the face. This tactic of taking a break has worked for me time and again over the years.

Any time I'm overwhelmed and can't seem to find a solution, I can usually take a break for a while, work on something else, or take a day or two off. When I come back, my perspective is fresh and the solution generally is quickly and plainly within view.

The Effortless Flow

I've often heard and even said myself, "If it's from the Lord, it will just flow." Generally, this is a true statement. If you're having to jump through hoops, force events and circumstances or impatiently maneuver other people to get what you want then it's either not what God wants you to have or the timing isn't quite right. Nine times out of ten if it's a righteous desire, then the timing is just off. You probably haven't collected all the pieces for the puzzle to come together.

An example of this is a book that I'd wanted to write for my dad for about twelve years. Off and on, we'd talk about a book that would inspire Americans to love their country, value the U.S. Constitution, and go back to the fundamental principles upon which the U.S. was built. But nothing ever seemed to materialize. We couldn't decide on a format for it or who the target audience would be. Over time, I learned the ins and outs of publishing books. In the summer of 2002, I became interested in family history and started studying the Revolutionary War period because of my fourth great grandmother, a Revolutionary War heroine, for whom I felt a particular kinship. I asked my dad to bring to my house all his books on this time period so I could study about the era. I was contemplating a novel about her life. About the same time, I'd decided to compile a quote book for Christian parents.

On a Wednesday evening, I had just finished the Christian parents quote book and had it ready to proofread. I sat down and read through some history books about the Revolutionary War, then I hopped into the shower. Then it hit me, "Compile a patriotic quote book and dedicate it to your father." The idea came with such force and intense desire that I knew beyond a shadow of a doubt that it would happen. The next morning I got on my knees and asked Heavenly Father to lead me to the quotes that should be included in the book. I began going through my father's books page-by-page. If the Spirit said to include it, I included it. On Friday afternoon, I emailed a copy of the book to my parents to proofread. My dad loved it. Saturday my parents came to my house with the corrections. Monday I sent the manuscript to the printers and by Thursday I had a printed copy of the book in my hands. One week from conception to fruition! For me, it was nothing short of a miracle.

While this book was years in contemplation, when all the pieces came together and the timing was right, everything just flowed effortlessly into place. Success is when preparation meets opportunity.

Forging Ahead Against the Odds

There are other times that it is important for you to forge ahead into the unknown. Everything may not fall effortlessly into place for you.

Something you want dearly may require a leap of faith. Sometimes you'll have to abandon your vehicle and get out and walk. The Lord may be telling you that it is time for Him to carry you in His arms through a swampy terrain. If He tells you to take a detour or to forge ahead, then do it! Don't question, don't whine or complain, just do as instructed in perfect faith that His way is the very best way to collect the treasures you need.

The greater the leap, the greater the reward. At times the Lord will require you to step out into the darkness, into the unknown. He may require you to do things that aren't popular, that may not conform to the wishes of family members or friends. He may ask you to sacrifice something of great value so that you can obtain a treasure of greater value. Some treasures have a price attached.

The Revolutionary War patriot, Thomas Paine, wrote these stirring words about the need for sacrifice in obtaining celestial treasures:

"These are the times that try men's souls. The summer soldier and the sunshine patriot will in this crisis, shrink from the service of his country; but he that stands it now, deserves the love and thanks of man and woman. Tyranny, like hell, is not easily conquered; yet **we have this consolation with us, that the harder the conflict, the more glorious the triumph. What we obtain too cheap, we esteem too lightly; 'tis dearness only that gives everything its value. Heaven knows how to put a proper price upon its goods**; and it would be strange indeed, if so celestial an article as freedom should not be highly rated." (Thomas Paine, *The American Crisis*, no. 1, 1776)

If we wish to obtain a precious celestial treasure, there are times when we must be willing to forge ahead when others would shrink from the challenge. Think of the Israelites when they first sent spies into the Promised Land. The people believed the evil report of the 10 fearful spies and refused to believe Joshua and Caleb who knew that the Lord could easily overpower the giants and give them the land. Because the Israelites shrank back in fear and refused to take the leap of faith, they lost their chance to enter the Promised Land. Forty years passed while the faithless generation died off and only Joshua and Caleb remained of the original group to enter the land.

What if the American founding fathers had shrunk back and refused to pay the price of freedom? Where would Americans or even the world be today? The Savior taught of a rich man who when he found one solitary pearl of great price sold all that he had that he might obtain that one pearl. Some celestial treasures are worth any price that is asked.

The Lord will periodically navigate you into seemingly hopeless situations where you are required to take a leap if you would obtain a glorious treasure. He never forces you to jump. There is usually a back door through which you may slink away. But if you refuse to leap at that point, you will lose the chance for that treasure for a season. Like the Israelites, you will be doomed to wander until you can collect enough faith and trust in the Lord to face Jordan again. Remember, some opportunities may never come again.

Circles
by Marnie L. Pehrson

I keep going round in circles.
Will this challenge never end?
Why do my trials repeat themselves?
Not much more can I withstand!

Then I call upon the heavens.
God's grace attends as I pray.
The lesson becomes crystal clear:
My thoughts do me betray.

I have expected to go in circles.
In my heart I did not believe
That anything could be different
And so my trials did I relive.

Now I will envision better paths
For my successful life to take.
In time I will expect the best and
A better life my thoughts will make.

For as a man thinketh
In his heart of hearts is he.
God grants according to desires.
What we expect will certainly be.

Chapter 6
Are You Going in Circles?

"Where there is no vision, the people perish but he that keepeth the law, happy is he." - Proverbs 29:18

I mentioned earlier that God enjoys taking us back to our beginnings – as He did by taking me back to my friend in Florida before embarking on a new period of spiritual growth. But sometimes, God isn't the one taking us in circles. It's we who are chasing our own tails.

Sometimes we get stuck in a pattern of repetitive behavior. We're like the children of Israel wandering around in the wilderness. The only reason we're wandering in circles is that we haven't learned what we need to learn to break free and move on.

In order to explain why we do this and how to break this pattern, we have to understand how our minds work. Proverbs

23:7 tells us that as a man "thinketh in his heart, so is he." Notice this verse doesn't say, As a man "thinketh in his head, so is he." Our conscious mind may have one set of ideas, but our subconscious mind (our heart) is still stuck in a rut.

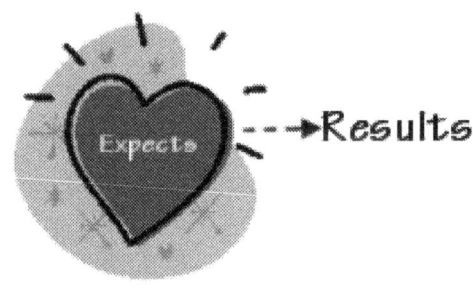

Whatever you expect in your heart is what you get. You may talk your head into believing that you're going to change or that you want a new level of abundance, but if your heart doesn't really believe it, you'll keep getting what you're getting. For example, if your heart expects to be hurt in relationships, you will keep getting hurt. If your heart expects to be in debt, then you will continue a cycle of debt. (See my family's story in Chapter 3.)

Psalm 37:5 says, "Delight thyself also in the Lord; and he shall give thee the desires of thine heart. Commit thy way unto the Lord; trust also in him; and he shall bring it to pass."

The Lord grants unto us according to the desires of our heart. Whatever your heart really believes that it can achieve and expects to receive is what – by law – you will receive. God will gradually lead you so that you will wake-up and realize what is happening, but He will not intervene and force your will. He won't stamp His imprint upon the human heart unless that heart wants to be "stamped."

The expectations of your heart determine your results. If you want different results, then your heart has to change. The message has to get down into your heart and change what your heart expects. Otherwise you'll just keep seeing your present results and expect that that's the way it's got to be and you'll keep repeating the same old habit patterns.

Breaking the Cycle

The way you break the cycle is to feed your heart a new idea. Your heart doesn't have the ability to accept or reject an idea, but with your conscious mind, you can decide what you will allow your heart to accept or reject. You can filter what gets down into your heart.

With your conscious mind you can formulate a new idea – a new picture of the way you want your life to be. You are a creative, spiritual being – created in the image of your Heavenly Father. If you want to break a chain of abuse,  debt, obesity, disease, addiction or stress all you need to do is create a new picture of yourself free from the situation. Create a new idea, nourish it into spiritual form and eventually it will manifest itself in the physical world. God creates everything spiritually before He creates it physically. This is where faith comes in… an eye of faith will see the things which are true that are not visible to the physical eyes. An eye of faith will hold onto the fact that your desires are taking shape and that they are present with you in spiritual form. Once you begin to formulate your new idea, think of it as being spiritually created in the room with you. It's there. You just can't see it with your physical eyes. It's like a seed planted in the earth or a baby in its mother's womb. Just because you can't see it, doesn't mean it's not there (See Ecclesiastes 11:5). Faith is patient and waits for the spiritual to grow into the physical. Just as we can't see a bean seed sprouting under the earth, we still have faith that eventually it will emerge from the earth, grow and bear fruit. The same process works with your ideas as they transform into spiritual and then physical form. Every seed has an assigned germination period. We know from experience the germination period of garden seeds, but we just haven't learned the germination periods for ideas. Be patient and give it time.

Visualization Tools

Your heart most likely will not immediately believe what you're feeding it. So you have to drown out the old expectations and impress new ones upon your heart. Here's how you do that:

Daily or even more frequently, in a relaxed state of mind, paint a picture of the life you desire. Write it down, develop real gratitude for it. Each day spend some time catching the vision of your new life, and then write down on paper what you envision. Write it in this way, "I am so happy and grateful now that ..." Follow this with whatever you know that the Lord wants for you. Paint a picture on paper of the vision the Lord has given you. Pray with gratitude for the things you know the Lord has on the way for you. Then, listen closely for the prompting of the Holy Ghost as it gives you directions for accomplishing your goals. *You take care of "what" you put into your heart, and allow God to take care of "how" it is accomplished.*

A good friend of mine who has overcome bad habits in the past has used what she refers to as "positive self-brainwashing." She decided that if media and environment could talk her into believing that drugs, cigarettes and alcohol would make her cool, successful and happy, then positive media and environment could help turn her around. Over a period of several years, she began a systematic method of filling her mind with the positive. She continually looked for positive phrases, scripture verses and quotes and put them on index cards, posters and signs that she placed around her house and carried with her to help remind her of positive uplifting things. She immersed herself in the scriptures and good books and leaned on the Lord in prayer.

She explained "If you don't fill your mind with something, then someone else will fill it for you." One of the most compelling things she has ever done to go forward in becoming the person that God intends has been to create a collage of the person she wanted to be. She went through magazines and took words, pictures and phrases that represented the person she wanted to become and put them on a poster in a collage. Today, years later, she still has that original poster and she has become the confident, self-assured, addiction-free individual that she visualized and represented on this poster. Even though her environment was the total opposite of what she wanted to be, that vision of *who* she wanted to be transformed her from the inside out. Not only has she changed, but also in her changing she has been an instrument in the hands of God to transform the lives of those around her – pulling herself and her children out of a depressing environment to one filled with hope and promise. She spends her days looking for opportunities to share what she's learned with others who are hungry for something better for their lives.

She explained, "It is important any time that we want to make a major change in our lives to get a clear picture of who we want to be when we reach our goal. You need to define where you want to go. People are usually visual. When you're in doubt, when you're having a bad day, and all the work you've done seems fruitless – look at the poster and remind yourself of what you're shooting for."

"You're planting seeds within your own mind of who you want to be. If you don't you're leaving it up to a chaotic world to plant whatever it wants in there."

All of this process – of collecting and displaying uplifting quotes, pictures and verses is helping you discover what is important to you and what you stand for. It gives your life meaning, purpose and direction. "You've got to find out who you are and what you stand for. You don't know where you're going or what you're bending for if you don't know what you stand for."

I challenge you to start today. Sit down with some magazines and pull out words, pictures and phrases that represent who you want to become, what you want to have in your life, and what you want to do with your time. Create your poster. The interesting thing about this process is that it's not that you are becoming anyone foreign. You are discovering who you really are inside. It's like Michaelangelo said when he was sculpting David. He didn't sculpt or create David. David was already in there, and Michaelangelo simply "set him free."

With God's help, you will be set free. You can become who you really already are inside. The kingdom of God is within you. (Luke 17:21)

Act As If

Once you have a clear picture of the person you'd like to be and the things you would like to have and do, begin to act as if you are already that person and are already doing the things you want to do. If your family car is falling apart and you can't consistently get to church on Sundays, then create a mental picture of the car you desire, shop around and test-drive cars to find the exact model you want. Take a picture of yourself next to the type of car that you want. Visualize yourself driving it to church, school and work. When you're driving your clunker, mentally picture yourself in the new automobile. Feel what it would be like to not worry about whether the car would start in the morning or whether it would break down on the way home from work. Act as if you already have it. Thank the Lord that He has a new car on its way to you so that you can go where you need to go in safety and security. Soon, things will start to fall into place and the Lord will prepare the way for you to receive what you need.

If you have been under a lot of stress and have been snapping at your children a lot, and you would like to control your words and your temper, then begin to act as if you are a patient and gentle individual. Picture yourself responding kindly when you are under pressure. Picture yourself remaining cool and calm. Take a picture of yourself with your children when you are happy and peaceful. Put it up somewhere where you will see it often. In stressful situations, stop to pray for help to act the way the person you would like to be would act.

Act as if you already have the thing you desire and soon it will be yours. Act as if you are already the person you want to be, and soon you will become that person.

God Wants to Exalt You

It is important to understand that the Lord wants you to have abundance in your life. Many people think that God wants them to live in poverty or to be tied down in a humble situation. But this couldn't be further from the truth. The Lord only allows us to be abased and brought down to a humble state so that he can lift us up and exalt us. It is in our humble state that we learn to lean on Him. Once you surrender to Him, He can lift you up. But if you lean only on yourself, He'll never be able to do that for you, because you won't allow Him to.

My friend, Karon Thackston, author of *The Faith Process* is a successful copywriter and marketing expert. Anything she takes on seems to prosper right out of the starting gate. I have been impressed with her ability to integrate her love for our Heavenly Father with her business practices and to lean on Him to guide her steps. As a result, He has prospered her greatly.

If one were to ask Karon to describe one attribute of our Heavenly Father, she would say, "Father doesn't do anything small." Then she would quote Ephesians 3:20 and say that Father gives us "exceeding abundantly above all that we ask or think, according to the power that works in us." That power is the Spirit working through our faith and our agency to choose.

Karon has a philosophy of abundance that is well-documented in scriptures. And I believe that this verse that Karon claims is a critical factor in her business success. She doesn't think small. Karon thinks big because she knows that Father thinks big. She knows that Heavenly Father wants to bless her. She follows the law of the tithe and accordingly the windows of heaven are opened and blessings are poured out upon her head (See Malachi 3:10).

Not only that, but Karon is a team player. She understands Luke 6:38, "Give, and it shall be given unto you; good measure, pressed down, and shaken together, and running over, shall men give into your bosom. For with the same measure that ye mete withal it shall be measured to you again."

A person who believes in abundance is willing to share what she has with others. She is willing to tithe, to donate to worthy causes, to give her customers her very best, and to help others. This person knows that the laws of God dictate that those who give will have it returned to them in "good measure, pressed down, shaken together and running over."

People with scarcity mentalities limit their own ability to receive. Because they will not sow, they cannot reap. Jesus said, "The thief cometh not, but for to steal, and to kill, and to destroy: I am come that they might have life, and that they might have it more abundantly." (John 10:10)

Our Heavenly Father and His Son Jesus Christ want to bless you with abundance! When you obey God's laws you reap the natural consequences of those laws. When you receive any blessing, it is by obedience to that law upon which the blessing is predicated. Ignorance is no excuse. Just because a baby doesn't know about gravity doesn't keep gravity from acting upon him should he dive off a couch. Neither do the laws of God suspend themselves just because we aren't aware of them. As we study the word of God, we are led to understand important laws that govern God's universe. We learn that there is abundance in God's creations. The propensity to believe that God will deny us the things we need keeps us from obtaining all that He has to give us. We're not exercising the faith necessary to receive.

We may ask, but do we really expect to receive? James 1:5-6 emphasizes this aspect of asking and receiving: "If any of you lack wisdom, let him ask of God which giveth to all men liberally and upbraideth not, and it shall be given him. But let him ask in faith, nothing wavering, for he that waverth is like a wave of the sea driven with the wind and tossed."

If there are things that are lacking in your life, or if you keep finding yourself in the same distasteful situation, begin to believe that your Heavenly Father has more than enough and to spare to fulfill your needs and desires. He wants to bless you. He wants you to be freed from the cycle of bondage. Seek to understand His will for your life, and then exercise your faith in accordance with His will to ask, and to believe that He will answer with abundance. Envision what you desire and thank Him in advance for what you know He will provide.

Chapter 7
Cast Thy Bread Upon the Waters

"Give, and it shall be given unto you; good measure, pressed down, and shaken together, and running over"
- Luke 6:38

I have come to love the wisdom of Ecclesiastes. Chapter 11, in particular, is a rich tutorial on the principle of sowing and reaping, otherwise known as the Law of the Harvest, or in the vernacular, "What goes around comes around." My closest friends embody this principle in their lives. They generously give. In business, they are "team players" and realize that if we expect to receive, we must first give. We have to make room for the things we seek *before* we can receive the new we desire.

Ecclesiastes 11:1 explains, "Cast thy bread upon the waters: for thou shalt find it after many days. Give a portion to seven, and also to eight; for thou knowest not

what evil shall be upon the earth." In other words, put out good, help others, and it will return to you in your hour of need. If you have sown good seeds, then in your moment of crisis, it will return to your rescue in the exact moment that you need it. While spending a day with my friend and mentor, Leslie Householder, I realized that had I never started SheLovesGod, then in my moment of crisis, this dear friend never would have found me. She held the answers to my prayers, but I never would have received those answers if there had been no SheLovesGod site for her to stumble upon in her moment of trouble. We simply never would have met. If you don't cast your bread upon the waters, it can't come back to you when you need it most.

Whatever you put out, by eternal law, has to come back to you. Ecclesiastes emphasizes the certainty of this principle with two comparisons, "If the clouds be full of rain, they empty themselves upon the earth: and if the tree fall toward the south, or toward the north, in the place where the tree falleth, there it shall be." As surely as heavy clouds send forth rain and as surely as you'll find the tree where it fell, so assuredly will you reap what you have sown.

There is a time to sow and there is a time to reap, but you don't do both at the same time. You can't be certain when or from where you'll reap, but reap you shall. Most likely the person to whom you give, will not be the one to return your kindness. This is where most people trip up. They think they have to get back from the exact person to whom they gave, and that simply isn't the way this law works.

Ecclesiastes 11:4 says, "He that observes the wind shall not sow; and he that regards the clouds shall not reap." In other words, those who are so preoccupied with only what they can see – their current circumstances – will not put forth the effort to sow or to reap. The fact that they can't see how they're going to benefit will discourage them. So they'll do nothing. Because they will not sow, they cannot reap. Your job is to send out good, and God will take care of the rest. Verse 5 compares the mystery of this principle to a child growing inside a mother's womb: "As thou knowest not what is the way of the spirit, nor how the bones do grow in the womb of her that is with child: even so thou knowest not the works of God who maketh all."

God takes what we sow and transforms it into abundance. Just as a tiny pea yields a plant laden with peas, so the Lord takes our efforts and multiplies them in our behalf. We can never be certain when, where or what seeds we sow will yield a harvest. But verse 6 admonishes us, "In the morning sow thy seed, and in the evening withhold not thine hand: for thou knowest not whether shall prosper, either this or that, or whether they both shall be alike good." In other words, cheerfully do all within your power to lift, to build, to help and to serve from morning until evening, because you never know when or how your blessings shall return.

Have you ever spent 10 minutes arguing with a friend about who was going to pay the tip at a restaurant, or over the price of a gallon of milk that you wanted to give her, but she insisted on paying for? If we understood the principle that one cannot give without receiving, we wouldn't quibble over a few dollars. We'd graciously accept what someone wanted to do for us or give us because we'd know that our friend would be blessed over and above what s/he gave. I'm not saying to be a free-loader, nor to let other people pay your way all the time, but if someone insists upon giving you something, then don't deny them the blessing of giving!

When you have something you don't need anymore, give it away, don't sell it. If you sell it, the money will be all you receive in exchange. But if you give it away, it will come back to you in a far greater way. Jesus taught, "Give, and it shall be given unto you; good measure, pressed down, and shaken together, and running over, shall men give into your bosom. For with the same measure that ye mete withal it shall be measured to you again." (Luke 6:38)

If you want a new couch, call Salvation Army to pick up the one you have. If you want new clothes, clean out your closet and give the ones you don't wear or that don't fit to a charity. Make room for the things you desire by giving away the old and making room for the new. Don't be afraid that you won't receive. By law you have to. I challenge you to try an experiment. Pick something around your house that you would like to have replaced. Give it away and see what God brings you in its place. I think you'll be pleasantly surprised.

Chapter 8
Cast Not Away Thy Confidence

"Cast not away your confidence, which hath great recompense of reward." - Hebrews 10:35

The Red Sea loomed ahead of them, desert lay on either side and Pharaoh's army approached from behind. The children of Israel were in a position of peril with nowhere for escape – or so it appeared. Immediately they cried to Moses, "would that we had stayed in Egypt." But Moses knew that the Lord didn't bring them this far to let them be slaughtered. In answer to his prayers, the Lord revealed to Moses a way of escape. It was something that had never been done before, but that didn't matter. Moses would hold out his staff and the Red Sea would part in half. The Israelites would cross over on dry sea bottom and

Pharaoh's armies would be swallowed up when the waters returned to their former state.

Just because no one had ever parted the Red Sea before didn't mean it couldn't be done. Similarly, just because your circumstances may seem bleak, it doesn't mean that God doesn't have a solution for you that has never been tried before. Miracles happen every day for those who have the faith to believe.

When the Lord reveals a direction to you, it will come as a feeling of peace and comfort. This is a sign from the Spirit of the Lord. That is why Jesus referred to the Holy Ghost as the Comforter. In John 14:26-27 Jesus promised, "But the Comforter, which is the Holy Ghost, whom the Father will send in my name, he shall teach you all things, and bring all things to your remembrance, whatsoever I have said unto you. Peace I leave with you, my peace I give unto you: not as the world giveth, give I unto you. Let not your heart be troubled, neither let it be afraid."

Fear, doubt, anxiety and worry do not come from the Lord. Feelings of peace, comfort and faith do. When praying about a decision, trust your initial feelings. If you initially feel a feeling of peace, comfort and warmth after praying, then the Holy Spirit is testifying to you that what you have prayed about is true and right. If your initial feeling after praying is doubt, fear, anxiety or confusion, then you may know that what you have prayed about is not God's will or is wrong.

The reason I say to trust your initial feelings is because if you inquire of the Lord and feel peaceful comfort concerning the matter, it is common to later experience feelings of doubt, fear or anxiety. This happens for three reasons. First, reality sets back in and what you see around you may contradict the answer the Lord gave you. If you're surrounded on all sides by the enemy, desert and water, then the natural mind is obviously going to be filled with doubt. If the Lord gives you a feeling of peace concerning a career decision, but circumstances say that it's not going to work out, then you may start feeling doubt or fear. If the Lord says your financial situation will be resolved, but bill collectors are calling you night and day, then it's natural to have feelings of anxiety or fear.

A second reason that you may later doubt your answer is that it is something totally new to your previous way of thinking. If the Lord reveals a new truth to you that goes against your previous conditioning, upbringing or preconceived notions, later you will experience anxiety, confusion and doubt about the truth of the principle. It takes time to adjust the programming of your mind to deal with new ideas. If you receive an initial confirmation of the truthfulness of a principle, don't let later doubts or frustrations get to you. Realize that it is only because your mind is having a hard time adjusting to the new principle. Stick with it, let it soak into your mind, study it, read and reread about it until it becomes a part of you.

A third reason that fear and doubt often follows the initial feeling of peace is that Satan doesn't want you to have faith. If what you have prayed about is important, then Satan will not want it to come to pass. He knows just as well as

God does that your faith is a key ingredient in the formula for a miracle. If he can fill your mind with doubt and fear, he can squelch the earlier vision of faith, cause you to give up and frustrate the situation.

Paul described this phenomenon in Hebrews 10:35 when he cautioned, "cast not away your confidence, which hath great recompense of reward."

I think the greatest disservice we do ourselves is forgetting or questioning the peace that the Spirit brings when we pray and get an answer. Being aware of the fact that later on you will probably feel doubt and fear about a situation helps you prepare for it.

Here are some tools for remaining confident in the vision of peace that the Lord has given you:

Seek the Spirit. Jesus taught that the Comforter speaks peace to our hearts and He brings all things to our remembrance – whatever the Lord has said to us. If you seek to live in harmony with the teachings of Jesus and seek to purify your life through Christ, the Spirit will become stronger in your life. The Spirit will help you remember the night you cried to the Lord and He spoke peace to your soul concerning the matter.

Write It Down. After you receive your answer, write down your thoughts and feelings. Document the answer you received from the Lord. Describe the vision of what it will be like and feel like when the answer to your prayer becomes a reality.

Envision Your Outcome. Take time each day to envision what your life will look like and feel like when your prayer is answered. Frequently review what you wrote down after you received your answer. Pray to the Lord and thank Him for what He is doing and is about to do in your life.

Keep Your Eyes on Christ. Sometimes I get very overwhelmed with all the things on my plate, but there is a verse that I keep in front of me that brings me peace, "I can do all things through Christ which strengtheneth me" (Philippians 4:13). Also, I surround myself with pictures of Christ. By looking at these, it is as if He is saying to me *"Look to me in every thought. Doubt not, fear not."*

Expect Opposition. Anyone who has ever tried to make a difference has had those who jeered, ridiculed or fought against them. People made fun of Columbus, Edison, Noah, and Jesus Christ Himself. Expect people to tell you that it can't be done. Ignore them and forge ahead with a vision of your end in sight. When you pray and receive an answer on anything of importance – on anything that will do some good in the world – Satan immediately attacks to shake our confidence. Don't let him. Go forward in faith despite the odds.

Don't Wait for Things to Be Perfect Before You Act. When the Israelites finally entered the Promised Land, they had to cross the Jordan River at its highest point. The Lord instructed the priests to carry the Ark of the Covenant toward the water's edge and step into the water and then the river would part. The priests did as instructed and stepped into the swollen river. Reminiscent of the Red Sea, the Jordan River parted and the people crossed on dry land. But the priests had to step forward in faith first. Similarly, the Lord may require you to step forward before a way is made for you.

The Lord likes us to take initiative. Don't wait for everything to be perfect before you do anything. Don't procrastinate. Do what you can do. I've found that if the Lord directs me to do something He always prepares a way for it to be accomplished. Even if I don't know how, if I forge ahead and do what I can do, the Lord reveals to me what I need as I go along. Trust the Lord enough to move forward even when you don't know how you can possibly accomplish it all.

Be Patient. Every seed has its own germination period to come to fruition. "To everything there is a season and a time for every purpose under the heaven" says Ecclesiastes 3:1. Don't become frustrated if things don't seem to be happening as fast as you'd like. Hang on in faith and endure to the end. You can control your faith and whether you act upon the instructions of the Lord, but you cannot control the timing of events. Have faith that the "the vision is yet for an appointed time, but at the end it shall speak, and not lie: though it tarry, wait for it; because it will surely come, it will not tarry…the just shall live by his faith" (Habakkuk 2:3-4).

Cast your mind back on the time when you prayed and received your answer. Lean on that. Don't question it. Walk on in faith and "cast not away your confidence, which hath great recompense of reward" (Hebrews 10:35).

In the Hollow of His Hand
by Marnie Pehrson

When thick storms gather blackness
When the thunder rolls overhead
When temptations claw around you
And you fear you'll lose your head

Call upon the heavens
Reach high and lift your gaze
And pray and wait patiently
For Jesus' smiling face.

For when life's challenges engulf you
And you call upon His name
He will never leave nor forsake you
Just wait patiently for his embrace.

In that moment of silence
Between decision and the dawn
Lies a world of darkness that claims
The light will never come.

Hang on; hold on; be still, my friend
For when the darkness flees and the light ascends.
You'll discover that you've been carried
In the hollow of His hand.

Chapter 9
The Due Time of the Lord

"To everything there is a season and a time to every purpose under the heaven." - Ecclesiastes 3:1

As I've said earlier, there are many things you can control in life, but timing is generally not one of them. It seems that life never delivers what we want when we want it. It's either too early or too late. But in reality, the Lord's timing is always perfect.

I like to think of any idea, dream or desire as a seed. Every seed has an assigned germination period. It must be planted, given time to sprout, grow, be nurtured, cultivated and eventually bear fruit.

The best analogy I've heard for this is an acorn. Does an acorn have an oak tree inside of it? It has the plan for an oak tree – right? It doesn't have everything yet,

but it has the blueprint or the promise of an oak tree inside of it. If you hold that acorn in your hand long enough will it grow or disintegrate? It will eventually disintegrate – right? If you want it to grow, you have to plant it in the right kind of soil. Then in time, the acorn will become an oak tree.

Does the acorn have to fight and claw to become an oak tree? No, it simply holds the blueprint of the tree in its cell structure and everything that it needs to become a tree is drawn to it out of the soil, air and water. In the appointed gestation period, the acorn becomes a tree.

Similarly, when we have the vision of a goal that the Lord has promised us, we can plant it in our minds, and hold the vision of it in faithful diligence with patience for the timing of the Lord. Diligence with your vision means you act on every prompting that you receive from the Spirit as you hold this vision. No matter how insignificant or silly it may seem, heed the promptings you receive from the Spirit and act immediately on them. From small and simple things are great things brought to pass.

On a recent occasion I was able to almost-effortlessly turn some ideas I had two years prior into a reality. I'm an idea person and have more ideas than I know what to do with. I easily become overwhelmed and run around like a chicken with its head cut off trying to do too many things at once. My former coach encouraged me to create a master list of ideas so that they were recorded for later reference. I've kept up this practice off-and-on over the last few years and when the opportunity and knowledge presented itself to turn those old ideas into a reality, I learned an important lesson.

Sometimes God gives us ideas whose time has not yet come. For example, many times ideas come to me with such force and in such a burst of light and knowledge that I know they didn't come from within me. There's no doubt that they came from God. I recognize these ideas because they fill me with joy. They are filled with light. But often, I become so frustrated because at the time they come, I may not have the means or the knowledge to make them a reality. So reluctantly I file the idea back into a corner of my mind and eventually the time, season and purpose for that work presents itself.

In this instance, a programming problem arose on one of my Web sites that required immediate attention. I had to quickly research a solution and repair the problem. In my moment of need, the Lord led me to a piece of programming code that not only fixed the current problem, but also gave me the knowledge to quickly and easily implement the ideas He gave me two years prior. Within a week's time those ideas became a reality. They were there waiting for their time and their purpose.

What I learned from this experience is that we need not question the inspiration or answers we receive because the way or means to accomplish them are not immediately available. Sometimes the Lord gives us this insight so that we

1. have a direction to pursue,
2. can accumulate the knowledge and experience the idea requires, and
3. can be on the lookout for the opportunity when the perfect time arises. Often that opportunity is hidden within a crisis.

We need not be discouraged because we can't do everything we want to do right now. We can take comfort in knowing that the Lord has a time and a purpose for every righteous desire that He puts within our hearts.

The hard part for us humans is having the patience to wait for God's perfect timing. We often try to force the issue. But our own efforts to manipulate a situation to change the foreordained timing of events will only end in frustration. In God's timing, events just flow. Don't force things. Forcing things generally ends up undermining the very thing you seek.

The timing of inspiration and fruition don't always coincide. You can console yourself in knowing that the inspiration and vision He showers your way today will eventually become a reality - even if it's in a distant tomorrow. Document enlightenment as it comes, and praise Him when its season arrives.

Remember the acorn. The question for us to ponder is no longer *how* or *if* we will receive the promised blessing; it is simply a matter of *when*. Knowing with this level of assurance that you will receive the promise gives you an amazing level of patience to wait for God's perfect timing. Most importantly, you learn to listen to and trust the Spirit. Ultimately God is in control of everything! You just hold the vision and follow instructions. Like the acorn, there is no need to fight, manipulate or force the outcome. You simply trust the Lord to let things flow and respond when prompted.

The following true story, told by my friend Mia Cronan of MainStreetMom.com, illustrates how God's timing and plans are always the best timing.

Have you ever been smacked in the head with the sudden realization that your perception of things does not bear even a close resemblance to reality? We think we know the deal; we think we understand everything we need to do to build a successful life, free of problems, as long as things go our way. (Therein lies the problem.) It's hard to fathom that, in spite of the fact that we live spiritually upright lives, use morally strong judgment, and make maturely principled decisions, things do not always go our way.

Such was the case for me through most of the year 2002. Early in the year my husband was in the throes of searching for a job, one more suited to his credentials, accomplishments, goals, and lifestyle. In other words, this would be a job where he could use his brain instead of merely his patience. My husband is a very talented and knowledgeable man, and his position at the time was not a good fit for him. He had been trying for over two years to secure a new position within his company, but he had yet to gain the experience he needed to be ready for it.

Mid-March of that year, he interviewed for a position in Green Bay, Wisconsin and flew back to Pennsylvania from the interview looking war-torn and beaten. He could not believe the rigor with which they drilled him, and he was sure he was promptly crossed off the list of candidates the minute he was out the door. His words were, "Don't worry, honey, we're not moving to Green Bay." Not much of a cold winter person, I was quietly pleased, feeling as though we had dodged a bullet.

The very next day, I came home from running errands, only to find him here at home when he would normally be at work. He met the children and me at the door with a big grin on his face. The company loved him! He'd been offered the job and wanted to get my take on the idea. We discussed it and agreed...it's best for his career to accept the position. There would be a slight change in the pay structure, and the benefits were not quite as good, but the experience was something he had been needing for a while, so that he could move in a new direction within his industry. He accepted the position, and agreed to start two weeks from that day. Immediately, we listed our home, confident it would sell promptly and that we could all be together soon. Our four children and I stayed back to oversee the home sale, the move, and to allow them to finish the school year in Pennsylvania. We prayed constantly as a family that our home would sell quickly so that we could be together again. I prayed constantly in private that I could keep things together by myself without falling apart. I knew in my heart of hearts that we would be fine, that God would provide, and that He had a big plan for us, one over which I had no control, which was very hard for me. And I was very sad about leaving friends and struggled with the notion of saying goodbye.

My husband left to start his new job, unsure when we would see him again, because he would be afforded no vacation for one year. After three weeks of our home being on the market, yet no potential buyers having come through, we started to get concerned. Then the school year ended, and there was still no buyer, in spite of a smattering of lookers. The market was not in our favor. The children and I remained in Pennsylvania through the summer, since the house was not selling. The stress of the situation was compounding daily, and we knew that my husband's temporarily living stipend was about to dry up, meaning added stress from financially maintaining two homes. Having to keep the house buyer-ready at all times while raising our four children in it was hair-raising, at best. We continued to pray fervently, knowing that our prayers were being heard, but unsure as to why they weren't being answered.

Finally, in October (yes, the children started the new school year back at their old school, much to the surprise of the administration and all involved), we had had enough of being apart. In the six months that my husband had been gone, we had seen him five times. He missed us, we missed him, and he was missing out on the first year of our youngest child's life, among many other things. I withdrew the children from their school, we packed up the bare necessities and moved up to Green Bay to live in a tiny two-bedroom apartment with my husband. As long as we had to pay a mortgage and rent, why not be together? The kids were placed in a lovely school there and made some new friends. We registered at a church, got the kids going in religion classes, and continued to pray for a sale on our home. We were also assured by dozens of bystanders that we were in their prayers, too.

We sought and found the perfect rent-to-own situation and were thrilled at the notion of getting into a house and retrieving all of our belongings from Pennsylvania, even though our home had not sold yet. However, at the very last minute, the deal fell through, and we were heartbroken. We had thought for sure our luck was turning and things would start falling back into place. We were starting to wonder why we seemed to have a black cloud over our heads, because nothing seemed to be going right for us since the onset of the whole situation. We wondered where we had gone wrong in our lives. We try to be good folks and treat others like we like to be treated, etc. The children prayed with us as a family every single night to make our home sell so that we could be settled, but nothing seemed to be working. Financially it was getting harder and harder every month.

After having been in the apartment for about two months, my husband was talking to a friend of his from a company with which he had interviewed two years ago. This person knew of a position within my husband's old company, much like the job my husband was doing in Green Bay. After a great deal of correspondence resulting in an interview, my husband was offered and he accepted a job in Ohio, in his home town where he has family, two hours from our home in Pennsylvania, which still had not sold. So five days before Christmas, we packed up, and the children and I moved back into the house. My husband would commute from Ohio to Pennsylvania on weekends, coming home every Friday night, and living with his brother rent-free during the week!

This is where it gets interesting. Bear with me while I take a moment to point out a few things before I get to the crux of my message. First of all, my husband was more qualified for this position with his old company, because he had taken the job in Green Bay. Second of all, we would never have been able to even consider this opportunity, had the deal with the rent-to-own home not fallen through. Third of all, had our home sold when we wanted it to sell, we would be permanently in Green Bay, 12 hours from the closest family members. Additionally, he got his 15 years of seniority back, four weeks of vacation, more money, and our health insurance was reinstated with no waiting period.

And lastly, after coming back to Pennsylvania, we had a sales contract for our home in our hands within seven days. Yes, after ten months of waiting, it took seven days to sell our home after we left Green Bay.

It is my belief that God wanted us to go to Green Bay, but He didn't want us to stay there. He knew exactly what to do and when to do it. Naturally, I didn't see it at the time we were going through it...how could I? Clearly, He knew better than we did. God had the pieces of the puzzle in place years ago throughout my husband's career journey and in terms of whom he was in contact with along the way. He put the right people in the right places at the right times.

In looking back on it, I remember feeling profoundly faithful that things would work out eventually, and at the same time, deeply frustrated over the lack of control that I had. It was a very lonely period of time, too.

So, the movers will be here two weeks from today, and we will be on our way to our new life, in my husband's home town, as members of the church where he and his family grew up, where he and his brothers were altar boys. Our children will attend the same schools my husband attended and where their grandmother taught for years, and they will check out books from the same library where he did. We will be less than four hours from my family, down the street from my husband's brother and his family, and much closer to other out-of-town family members.

What have I learned from all this? Here goes....

- God has a plan and if we let Him handle things, the outcome can be dazzling.

- No matter how "on the ball" we are, things are sometimes meant to go in an unconventional direction to get you to the next destination.

- There is no place for anger in a trying situation, only faith and hope. Patience helps, too, but I don't naturally excel in that area.

- Things don't always turn out the way we planned, and often it is best that way.

- We have to allow ourselves the creativity in our lives to deviate from what we think is the right progression of events, because we don't have all the facts, nor are our priorities always in accordance with God's.

- We have to be willing to let God lead the way because He's got a much better view of the road ahead.

"A lamp unto my feet is your word, a light to my path." (Ps. 119:105)

Chapter 10
Amazing Grace

"He that abideth in me, and I in him, the same bringeth forth much fruit; for without me ye can do nothing... If ye abide in me, and my words abide in you, ye shall ask what ye will, and it shall be done unto you."
- John 15:1-7

Many people ask me how I juggle so many projects and raise six children. From my perspective, I feel like a jack of all trades and master of none. But others see what I do in a much different way. How can this be? I am convinced that it is the grace of God that takes my meager, scattered and feeble efforts and magnifies them for His purposes.

When we are in a covenant relationship with Jesus Christ, He is our partner and we have access to His enabling grace. Most people think of grace as the power that saves – the atoning power of Jesus Christ. This is true, but His grace plays more than a final saving role in our eternal existence. It plays a much bigger role in the lives of believers.

Through Grace the Impossible Becomes Possible

Grace is an enabling power. Jesus taught, "The things which are impossible with men are possible with God." (Luke 18:27) How are they possible? Through His grace! Grace is the power by which God can work His will in your life. It is the power that allows ordinary people to do extraordinary things.

The concept of grace is outlined in Ephesians 2:8-10:

"For by grace are ye saved through faith; and that not of yourselves: it is the gift of God: Not of works, lest any man should boast. For we are his workmanship, created in Christ Jesus unto good works, which God hath before ordained that we should walk in them."

Because on our own we fall miserably short, our works cannot save us; but the purpose of God's grace is to recreate us in Christ so that we can walk in good works. It is important to note that God gives us grace so that we can do His works and build His kingdom. A natural outflow of being in a state of grace is an abundance of good works (also referred to as "bearing fruit").

In the parable of the vine, Jesus explains that those branches that bear fruit are purged so that they may bear even more fruit. Many times the events that are most painful in our lives are God's purging process enabling us to bear more fruit (do greater works) (See John 15:1-7).

No matter how bad something appears to be, there is something of equal or greater good within it. The financial crisis I mentioned at the beginning of this book led me to priceless friends and information that increased my faith to a level I never thought possible. It enabled me to find total peace in trying circumstances. Without this hurdle, I never would have learned this life-transforming information. For me, it was worth the price. God's pruning helped me bear more abundant fruit.

Jesus said, "*Abide in me, and I in you. As the branch cannot bear fruit of itself except it abide in the vine; no more can ye, except ye abide in me. I am the vine, ye are the branches: He that abideth in me, and I in him, the same bringeth forth much fruit; for without me ye can do nothing... If ye abide in me, and my words abide in you, ye shall ask what ye will, and it shall be done unto you.*" (See John 15:1-7)

Without Christ's enabling grace, you can do nothing. With His grace, nothing that is God's will is impossible for you. You can ask what you will and it will be done. What a promise!

Activating God's Grace

According to Paul, each of us has different God-given gifts distributed according to the grace that is given to us. We activate and magnify these gifts "according to the proportion of our faith." (Romans 12:6)

Faith in Jesus Christ is the beginning. Following faith is humility and repentance. James

4:6 says, "God resisteth the proud, but giveth grace unto the humble." We activate God's grace by recognizing our own nothingness, our own inability to solve our own problems. You must come to a point where you surrender your will to God's will – where you realize that His way is the blessed way. Almost always, this realization comes while you are being "pruned."

Self-confidence must be replaced with faith. The wonderful thing about grace is that it is irrelevant how talented, weak or human you may be, God's grace is sufficient to make you strong. If you lean only on yourself, you see your own weakness and think, "I'll never be able to do that. I can't commit because I know I'm weak and I'll just mess up." But when you put your faith and trust in God, you can say, "Even though I am weak, I have faith that God will make me strong. I can do all things through Christ who strengthens me" (Philippians 4:13).

It is in your extremities that you become humble enough to look to God and surrender to Him. It is when you wholeheartedly commit to

Him and His will and surrender your control of the situation that you activate God's grace in your behalf. It is at this point that although you are weak, through Christ's grace you become strong.

As you replace self-confidence and your need-to-control with faith in the Lord Jesus Christ, you activate His powerful grace in your behalf. (Romans 12:3) With this grace, "no good thing will be withheld from *you* as *you* walk uprightly." (Psalms 84:11)

Grace "builds you up, and gives you an inheritance among all those who are sanctified." (Acts 20:32) "Come boldly unto the throne of grace, that *you* may obtain mercy, and find grace to help in time of need" (Hebrews 4: 16). "Grow in grace and in the knowledge of our Lord and Savior Jesus Christ." (2 Peter 3:18) As you lean on Him, your best efforts will no longer fall short because through the power of His grace, your weaknesses become strengths and the impossible becomes possible. I bear solemn witness that when we do our best to do God's will and lean on Christ's grace, He always makes up the difference.

Conclusion

Just as there are rules to the road when traveling across country, there are eternal or natural laws that God abides by when He interacts with His children. If we understand these rules of life and live in harmony with them, we will understand the pattern of our lives. Life won't seem so random and unfair when we understand the rules of the road. The following are a few of those rules that can make a big difference in your life:

1. **Circumstances "just are."** We make them good or bad by how we perceive them and how we relate to them. Often we use this rule against ourselves. We compare our weaknesses to other people's strengths or our lack of blessings in a particular area to another person's abundance. We should cease to compare our "treasures" with other people's and concentrate on the blessings that we do have. Each of us is unique with a customized path especially tailored to our needs.

2. **God grants us according to the desires of our hearts.** Our hearts control our destiny. Whatever your heart believes and expects is what you'll get.

3. **Seek a confirmation first.** Ask God if your path is right. If He confirms your course through the peaceful assurance of the Holy Spirit, then you may act in faith that your course is right. The seed you are planting is good. Forge ahead in faith.

4. **Faith is the substance of things hoped for, the evidence of things not seen.** Realize that God fashions your miracles from your faith. Cast away fear. Fear and doubt cannot occupy the mind simultaneously with faith. Faith propels your idea from a spiritual form to a physical form. Fear and doubt do the opposite. They send your idea back to the invisible.

5. **Gratitude boosts the signal of your faith.** Be grateful ahead of time for the things the Lord is sending and will send to you. Gratitude draws you nigh to God - the source of all

blessings - and plants your ideas into your heart.

6. **If you repeatedly encountering the same challenges, examine what your heart is expecting.** Exercise faith to visualize and impress upon your heart the new desired results.

7. **When embarking on any major change in your life, opposition is normal.** Forge ahead in faith. Don't let fear cause you to cast away your confidence. If the Spirit confirms your course is right, proceed against all odds. With God, nothing is impossible.

8. **Look for the good.** Within every bad circumstance is an equal and opposite good. If it's a little bad, then there's a little good laced within it. If it's catastrophic, then there's something phenomenal within it.

9. **This too shall pass.** There is a rhythm to life. When you hit a low point, realize that things

will get better. Sometimes there has to be void created to make room for the good that you desire to receive. This void may appear as a low point in your life, but really it's a blessing because it's making room for something new and better.

10. **You reap what you sow.** Give, serve and lift others at every occasion and in your moment of need, in unexpected hours you will receive - shaken, pressed down and overflowing. Reach out to others, they often hold the answer to your prayers.

11. **Every seed has a germination period.** There is a time to sow and a time to reap, but we don't do both at the same time. Realize that it takes time for your idea seeds to sprout, mature and bear fruit. The beginning of this process is invisible to the eye - it's a spiritual creation that can only be seen through the eye of faith. Have patience and wait for the seed to sprout. Then nourish it with all your might, mind and strength until it bears fruit.

12. Don't attempt to force the Spirit. Your job is to plant good ideas in your mind, expect God's help, and follow through on inspiration. You are not to administrate the creative process. That is God's job. Let Him handle the "how" while you handle the "what." If things aren't flowing the way you'd like, have faith that God will not cause you to pass through anything that is not absolutely necessary for you to meet your righteous objectives.

Remember these rules as you proceed through this treasure hunt called mortality, and you'll begin to see the meaning in the madness, the fairness in the seemingly unfair. You'll be able to unlock the blessings that God has in store for you.

May the Lord bless and keep you as you seek to fulfill His divine plan for your life. May you have joy and wisdom to rejoice even among your afflictions. May your grateful and faithful heart unlock the treasuries that heaven has in store for you through the grace of our Lord and Savior Jesus Christ.

About the Author

Marnie and her husband Greg Pehrson are the parents of six children and live in North Georgia near Chattanooga, Tennessee. Marnie is the founder of multi-denominational SheLovesGod.com which hosts the annual SheLovesGod Virtual Women's Conference the 3rd week of October each year. She writes a weekly Bible study lesson which you may subscribe to for free on the site. She has served in many capacities within her church in presidencies of the women's Relief Society and children's Primary organizations, and also as a Sunday School teacher, pianist and family history consultant.

Marnie is also an internet developer and consultant who helps talented professionals deliver their message to the online world. She is the creator of IdeaMarketers.com, LocateACoach.com, PWGroup.com, BelieversAtWork.com, & PowerOfLearning.com, etc. Throughout her sites, Marnie seeks to build resources that help others discover, develop and utilize their God-given talents.

Marnie welcomes reader comments and may be reached at webmaster@SheLovesGod.com or by calling 706-866-2295

Other Books by Marnie Pehrson

10 Steps to Fulfilling Your Divine Destiny:
A Christian Woman's Guide to
Learning & Living God's Plan for Her
ISBN 0-9676162-1-2, 124 pages
Have you ever said to yourself, "I'd love to do great things with my life, but I'm just too busy, too untalented, too ordinary, too afraid, too anything but extraordinary"? Inside this book you'll learn how to reach your full God-given potential.

Journal/Workbook Companion for
10 Steps to Fulfilling Your Divine Destiny:
A Christian Woman's Guide to
Learning & Living God's Plan for Her
ISBN 0-9676162-2-0, 220 pages

Packets of Sunlight for Christian Parents
Compiled by: Marnie L. Pehrson
144 pages, paperback
ISBN 0-9676162-4-7
Brighten your day with inspiration for parents of tots to teens!

Packets of Sunlight for American Patriots
Compiled by: Marnie L. Pehrson
108 pages, paperback
ISBN 0-9676162-3-9
Let the founding fathers, reignite your love for freedom!

To order call 800-524-2307 or visit
www.SheLovesGod.com/bookstore

www.ingramcontent.com/pod-product-compliance
Lightning Source LLC
Chambersburg PA
CBHW031941070426
42450CB00005BA/307